THE

WORLD

OF

VALUE

By

Terence Sweeney

The World Of Value © Terence Sweeney

Disclaimer

National Library of Australia Cataloguing-in-Publication entry:

Creator:	Sweeney, Terence, author.
Title:	The World Of Value / Terence Sweeney.
ISBN:	978-0-6480637-4-2 (paperback)
	978-0-6480637-5-9 (ebook)
Subjects:	Finance.
	Financial security.
	Business.
	Wealth--Social aspects.
	Social values.

Published by Terence Sweeney and High Value Books.
www.highvaluebooks.com

For Jack, Jessica, Luke & Chloe

Table of Contents

Introduction

B usiness and people are probably the two things that I find to be the most fun in the world.

People, because we are so fascinating. Being human is a fun, but challenging, experience, and I love watching how we all cope with it.

Personally, I have always been on a quest for freedom. Balancing my desire for freedom and self-expression with my need to co-exist with others in the world is what I tend to struggle with most in life. How do I fully express myself and still relate to others? How do I be fully self-expressed and have others still relate to me? How do I express all the love and passion I have for life without everyone running away screaming?

I am also passionate about business. The world of business is, after all, about people. It is bringing together people to create value for other people. I have been around business since I was six years old and still find business fascinating. Particularly, given the speed in which the business world is changing. Technology, and the internet, have had an incredible impact on society and our ability to create wealth. For some people, this can be troublesome. A world that is constantly evolving can appear to be extremely challenging to people who have fixed views of how business and life work.

A dynamic world is fine by me. I hate fixed views. When we think of ourselves, our business, or our life from a fixed point of view, it usually keeps us stuck where we are. I don't like being stuck — I like to be fluid. The ability to have a fluid view of life is essential if you want to keep performing at a high level.

A friend of mine once asked a question: "What does it take to be a great leader?" After listening to a room full of people's answers, he said, "Maybe a great leader is someone who is always in an enquiry of what it is to be a great leader?"

I love this. As soon as you think you know what it is to be a greater leader, you are screwed. You stop thinking about what it is going to take to be a great leader. To be a great leader, you have to be in an ongoing enquiry of what it is to be a great leader.

So a great husband is someone who is always in the enquiry of what it is to be a great husband.

A great father is someone who is always in an enquiry of what it is to be a great father.

A great lover is someone who is always in an enquiry of what it is to be a great lover.

A great business person is someone who is always in an enquiry of what it is to be a great business person.

This last sentence is the source of this book.

This book is designed to deepen your enquiry of what it is to be a great businessperson and, along the way, a great human being.

If you have ever grappled in your relationship with money.

If you have ever had a question about your own value.

If you think that there could be a bigger context for wealth, or a greater context for business.

This book will greatly impact your journey.

Over the coming chapters, we are going to look at people's context for wealth. I want to demolish your current view of wealth and create a new view to re-define how the world of wealth occurs to you. Why? Because this new view will give you greater access to being wealthy.

We will look at the world of value; what it is, how it can be created, and how you can capitalise on the creation of it. How it impacts all of your life. Its relationship to the world of business and how it impacts our relationship with each other.

You will develop a stronger relationship to money. Why it is powerful. What it is and what it is not.

You will gain a new level of understanding of the world of business and a new capacity for success as a business person.

You will also increase the effectiveness of your ability to impact the world.

No matter where you are in your journey to understanding value, wealth and money, this book will move you forward in that journey.

More than anything, however, I want you to be wealthy, and I want you to be free.

I should warn you that getting value from this book will take some effort on your part.

It may challenge your current ways of thinking.

Good…keep reading.

There will be moments when you experience what I am saying as just plain wrong.

Good…keep reading.

There will be times when you experience the book as being plain annoying.

Good…keep reading.

It will be worth it.

My Journey

Parents

Money and wealth have always played a big part in my life. I was born in Dundee, Scotland, to parents who had both grown up in working class families. Although they didn't agree on everything, two things united my parents. The first was a commitment to family, and the second was a desire to create a better life for both themselves and their children.

The access to a better life for them was to make money. It makes sense. If you have more money, you have more freedom and more opportunities. Most of the world has a similar intention.

Neither of my parents had grown up in families who were business people. However, when I was five years old, and while both were working in full-time jobs and juggling a family, my parents decided to set up a market stall at one of the many open-air markets in Scotland. They first tried selling underwear, then underwear and toys, and then just toys. I remember as a child being asked to stand by the stall and watch out for people stealing – although it was probably more to keep me occupied than for my effectiveness as a security guard.

Over the next 30 years, my parents progressed from market stall to having multiple shops in and around my hometown of Dundee. At different times, they owned clothing stores, hairdressing salons, and were also active in property development. They had a great deal of success. As is often the case in business, however, it wasn't always plain sailing. They were learning on the job and there were many challenges. Being a part of that world was also a great learning experience for me.

My First Business

Growing up, listening and watching my parents was incredibly valuable. It was an awesome apprenticeship. I subconsciously absorbed a lot about business — about what worked and what didn't work and, at the same time, I was creating my own views.

At 21, I saw an opportunity to put what I had learnt into practice and started up a business of my own. The idea was to set up a baby goods delivery business. This was before packs of nappies were vacuum packed. The packs were enormous, and you would often see mothers trying to carry these big packs of nappies around the town centre whilst also pushing their prams and managing their children.

I worked out that I could buy the nappies from wholesalers and deliver them to a customer's home for less than the list price in the supermarket. When a parent has a new baby, they need to buy nappies at regular intervals for the next two years. This meant, if I gained a customer soon after the baby was born and took care of them, I would likely have that customer for two years. When I also included the sundry items that parents of babies need, it seemed like a good business model.

I found a supplier. I went out to a local housing estate one day, knocked on a door, and started telling people what I was offering.

By the end of that day, I had six clients, and my first business, "Diapers Delivered", was born. (I also considered the name "The Nappy Man". However, at 21, I decided it just wouldn't be cool to be known as "The Nappy Man").

I had great enthusiasm for the business. Over the next few months, I acquired many more customers and was making a good profit.

There was a moment for me when I could have taken the business to the next stage of growth, which would have meant leasing storage premises. I considered the option, however, I instead sold the business to a competitor and went off on my next adventure. For the next three years, I worked in sales for multi-nationals such as PepsiCo, Sally Hair & Beauty, and Schwarzkopf. This was great experience. Having grown up around small business, working for a multinational gave me a different view of business. It allowed me to see how business was also done on a corporate level. I have thought many times since, that this has been one of my strengths as a business person. Having created start-ups and been involved in multinational corporations, and other businesses at every stage in-between, has given me a depth of experience. It also allows me to understand what it will take to transition a business to the next level.

Coming to Australia

By the time I was 25, for the first time in my life, I was earning a lot more money than I was spending. I bought my first house, then I bought an additional investment property which I converted from a studio into a one-bedroom flat.

At this point, I reached a crossroads. I knew that if I kept building a life in Dundee it would make it more difficult to move away. Dundee was a great place to grow up. However, when I looked into the future, I couldn't see that it held the challenges I wanted, or gave me the depth of experiences I wanted.

It felt like something bigger was calling. I decided to go travelling and explore more of the world.

At this time, my brother, Craig, was working in Canada on a golf course; however, his contract was ending and he also wanted to travel more. We purchased two one-way flights to Bangkok, I rented out my properties, and we were off. I had a great time travelling with Craig. We spent two months travelling overland through Thailand, Malaysia, Singapore, and Indonesia. I remember spending two weeks over Christmas and New Years of 1994 in

Bali, hanging out on the beaches and partying. It was one of the most fun times of my life. Next stop was Australia, and on the 2nd January 1995, I landed in Sydney. I was 25.

The moment I arrived in Australia, I knew I wanted to live here. In the moment of stepping off the plane, I felt the heat and the humidity but, more than that, I felt the energy of the place. It felt like home. It was also incredibly spacious. I felt like I could do anything here.

I stayed in Sydney for four months working in odd jobs before continuing to travel around Australia. The more I saw of Australia, the more I fell in love with it. The place was beautiful.

In June of 1995, while sitting on St Kilda Beach in Melbourne in glorious sunshine, surrounded by beautiful people roller-blading next to the beach, I looked up at the apartments overlooking the water. I thought: "Wouldn't it be incredible to create a life out here? To have a business, a family and to live in one of the apartments overlooking the beach?".

At this time, I had a one-year visa with no option of becoming a resident. Little did I know that less than ten years later, I would be married in a park overlooking the same spot on the beach where I sat that day.

Residency

After my visa expired, I returned to the UK. My plan was to put as much money together as possible to make an attempt to live permanently in Australia.

During the next two years, I worked my butt off in sales, kept my expenses low, and used the money wisely. By the end of 1997, in total, I owned two houses, two apartments, and had also acquired a hairdressing salon along the way. This gave me enough of a base to head back out to Australia.

I sold one of the properties, which gave me funds to travel. The income from the other properties and the hairdressing salon also gave me enough funds that I would have a basic lifestyle without having to work.

In February 1998, I landed in Australia again. My main aim was to obtain Australian residency. However, I also had two other aims: one was to become qualified as a PADI Dive-Master; the other was to become qualified as a ski-instructor. I decided to tackle these two first, then work out the residency issue along the way. Becoming qualified as a Dive-Master took three months. Becoming a Ski Instructor took three back-to-back winters over one and a half years. Along the way, I had an incredible time.

It was between one of these back-to-back winters that I had a couple of months to kill and passed through Melbourne before heading down the Great Ocean Road and up to Uluru. Whilst looking to buy a camera in Melbourne, I connected with the assistant in the camera store. She was a girl named Angela. Over the next few months, we kept in touch and, after returning from a ski-season in Europe, I moved to Melbourne to spend time with her.

We lived together for a year, however, my visa status did not allow me to stay permanently in Australia. At this point, I had a four-year business visa, which meant I had to leave the country every three months. I would usually fly to New Zealand for one night then fly back the next day. In a two and a half year period, I had to leave the country 9 times. Eventually, the visa issue started to impact our relationship.

We separated and I had to confront the possibility of moving back to Europe. While considering my options, however, I found that if I went to study either accounting or IT in Australia, and completed the degree in two and a half years, I would have just enough points to apply for residency.

I enrolled in RMIT University in Melbourne, worked hard both in my studies and on myself, and completed my degree in two and a half years with Distinction. In 2004, I applied for, and obtained, Australian Permanent Residency.

After spending so many years with this intention, it was a real achievement to obtain residency status. On one hand, there was the satisfaction of achieving the result. However, more importantly, being able to live and work legally in Australia gave me the foundation on which I would create the next stage of my life.

Being Sixty

Soon after achieving residency status, a whole new world opened up for me. I became employed as the Business & Finance Manager in the Melbourne Centre of Landmark Education (a multinational training and development organisation). One day, while I was in one of the training programs, I had a revelation that caused me to consider the next period of my life.

I was listening to the centre manager talk about her experience of being sixty years old. As I listened to her speak, I realised that *I* was on my way to being sixty. I didn't just realise it in my head though. It was as if I fast forwarded to being sixty. It really hit me that one day I would be there, dealing with the physical, mental and emotional impact of being sixty.

It also hit me that, although I was 35 at the time, it wasn't that far away. When I had the experience of being fast forwarded to sixty, I also had a moment of connecting to the older version of me and asked him, "If you could talk to the thirty-five-year-old me, what would you say?"

The sixty-year-old me said "I would tell him to play full out and play full out now. Don't wait. Get married, have kids, have a business and be a seminar leader."

In the next moment, I turned around. Sitting behind me was a girl I had been casually dating. She looked at me and smiled. We were married less than a year later.

Back in Business

Getting married was a big step for me — it started a new level of the game. I became a seminar leader and a father. Next, I wanted to get back into business.

At this time, I had little financial resources. Most of these had been used up to pay my way through college. The fees for an international student were expensive, and I no longer owned my properties in the UK or the hairdressing salon. I did have desire though.

I made plans to set up a financial services business. However, given I had little money, I suggested to my wife that we both take part-time jobs so we wouldn't have to take any funds out of the business for the first year. I took a part time general manager role at a local educational college in Melbourne, and my wife took a part-time job handing out newspapers to people as they arrived at an inner city carpark.

After about a week in my role, however, I realised the college was in severe financial difficulty. I worked with the owner to try to sell the college, but there were no buyers. I then worked with him to try to give it away, but there was so much debt that no one was interested. I knew I could have an impact on the business, however, at the time, I wasn't really interested. It seemed like a lot of work for little gain. The college's branding was old, there was debt of around $400,000 and the business was going further behind each month. On top of that, the staff were almost paralysed by a lack of communication. The business did have some strengths though. The founder of the college had a great reputation in his field. The college had originally offered the first Diploma of Kinesiology in Australia – and likely the world. It also had a reputation for being cutting edge. When it came to facing the liquidation of the business, it struck me that a great many people would be impacted. Knowing that I could impact the business left me with a dilemma. Do I let the business follow its current path into liquidation, or do I step in and try to turn it around? I put together an acquisition plan, acquired the business and knuckled down to work. After making drastic changes to the staff, marketing, course materials, etc., the business began to turn around. Within 12 months, we were profitable.

The Way Up

Things began to go very well. Away from business, my wife and I now had two beautiful children, and I was also leading personal development programs to groups of up to 150 people.

A year later, I acquired 2,500 sq metres of great real estate in Melbourne CBD, at half the market rate, with an option to lease the whole or parts of the building to other businesses if needed. I also started to consider where I would take the business next. I could see only two options:

1. Grow the business; and
2. Exit the business.

By this time, I had relationships with many of my competitors and started discussing joint ventures. I also called up the CEO of Think Education, a subsidiary of seek.com – an ASX listed multinational. We met up and, over the coming weeks, he put forward a proposal to purchase the college and to lease the whole building at market rate. Everything was looking great. The image of sailing off into the sunset was firmly established in my mind.

The Way Down

The boat didn't make it to the sunset, however. The negotiations with Think Education dragged on longer than expected and, eventually, they didn't get the funding they were expecting. We were only fully utilising a third of the building, and I didn't take steps to sublease the building because I needed this to be empty to complete the deal with Think Education. The extra rent we were paying during this period to keep the whole building greatly impacted the business. On top of this, the government announced that it would offer funding for students to study at TAFE. Although this was great for the students, as it greatly reduced their fees, the government placed a cap on the fees that the educational institutions could charge. These capped rates were much less than our normal fees. This greatly reduced our ability to capitalise on the value we were creating.

After unsuccessfully negotiating with others to enter into joint venture agreements, I ended up negotiating terms for the management to purchase the business from me.

In the meantime, I had also developed health issues. There were serious problems with my digestive system that I had been ignoring for a number of years, and these needed addressing. Medical specialists said I had Crohn's disease and that I would be on medication for the rest of my life. At one point, I weighed 38 kilos. My wife thought I was going to die and called my mother in Scotland, who flew out just in case. Once I sold the business, however, I focussed on taking care of me and spent some quality time with family. I also cut lactose and gluten out of my diet as this intolerance seemed to be a major factor in my digestion issues. Since changing my diet, I have been healthier than at any other period of my life.

Balance

One of my desires prior to selling the business was that I wanted to spend one year off with my children — particularly with my son Jack who would be starting school in 12 months. I remember there being a moment when I knew that the next 12 months would be difficult in the business. I could continue to push the business through or sell it. I remember thinking, "What is more valuable to me? If someone were to offer me $1 million to miss that year with my son before he went to school, would it be worth it?" I decided it wasn't. I ended up spending three awesome years at home looking after my kids. There was one year of winding down, one year of really experiencing life at that slow pace, and one more to start winding back up again. It was one of the best periods of my life.

There was a great deal of development in this time, both personally and in the way I related to business. This period with family allowed me to look at many of the experiences in my life. To look at them and also question them.

I started meditating and enjoyed the experience of being connected to myself. I stopped drinking alcohol and caffeine, stopped eating gluten and lactose, cut down sugar, got rid of my television, re-evaluated my relationship, and started to look at the world from a new perspective.

An interesting thing happened when I cut the amount of external stimulus out of my life — I became very clear. First, I became much clearer about me, then clearer on those people around me. Finally, I began to see the world much more clearly.

I always knew I would get back into business again. However, I did not intend to jump straight in, nor did I want to get a traditional job. I wanted to start creating a business around who I really was.

One of the things I had noticed in my time with my family was that there were serious errors in the way I related to money. Money would come and go but, either way, it always occurred as something separate from me. There was a disconnection between myself and my wealth.

I also realised that this had impacted the business activities in my life. Business always occurred as fun and challenging, but still hard work. This led to strong bursts of activity, but the activity would not be sustainable. I realised that I now wanted to create a business that would allow for balance and that would grow with me in the long term — one that would allow me to create a life of real wealth.

Over the next few months, I developed an income coaching clients in the area of personal performance. This was a great way of stepping back into the workforce.

It was during one of these sessions with a client that I had one of the greatest breakthroughs of my life. I told the client that "Money doesn't make the world go around. Value makes the world go around." In that moment, the significance of what I had said really hit me, and I realised that value was *everything*. This is one of the great pleasures of coaching people. There are times when you listen to yourself talk and you think, "That is awesome. Who is saying that? Wherever it comes from, it is gold."

Over the next few days, I thought more about the world of value and, for the first time in my life, clearly distinguished the relationship between wealth, value and money.

Next was to test the commercial value of my ideas. I developed these distinctions into a 12-week mentoring program and, later, into formats for business and corporate clients. I was impressed by the positive impact the programs made.

I also started blogging weekly. I had some great feedback. However, the content of one particular post on the relationship between money, wealth and value elicited a strong negative reaction from a few people that were unknown to me.

When I looked at the post, I didn't understand why there would be such a strong negative reaction. The post made complete sense to me. This negative reaction was good news — I felt like I was beginning to hit a nerve.

That is when I decided that this was the direction in which I wanted to push forward. If people found this conversation reactivating, then this was probably the very area where I could create the most freedom for people.

I moved to consulting with business, further testing my ideas.

I also stopped blogging and started to prepare myself for a fight.

Success and Freedom

Since I had my own breakthrough in understanding the relationship between wealth, value and money, my experience of life has completely altered.

There is a new sense of freedom — and a new sense of power. I work when I want, with the people I want to work with, and on projects that inspire me. I also receive value according to the value I create.

In the past, the desire for success was always there, as well as the willingness to work for it.

That is not what was in the way of me having greater success.

I have since realised that what was in the way was something else. It was my context for wealth. More specifically, the way I saw the relationship between wealth, value and money.

My relationship to money and wealth was not unusual. It had been picked up from the conversations around me as I grew up. Listening to my parents, their friends and the shows we watched on television. The way that people generally talk about money in the world.

I was no different from most of the other people on the planet, and I probably had been more successful than most. My context for money was still screwed up. Most people's context for money is screwed up.

I realised that unless I shifted my context, nothing would alter. Nothing else mattered.

It is like being on a train line from Paris to Moscow and trying to get to Rome. You can travel as long as you want. You can ask people for advice. You can interview people who have been to Rome and ask them how they got there. You can say affirmations that validate how much you want to be in Rome but, the reality is, you can't get there while you are on a Paris to Moscow train line.

When I clearly saw my relationship to money — when I was finally able to understand how it all worked — that is when I gained a new experience of freedom, and a new access to wealth.

It is very likely that you are currently on the Paris to Moscow train line trying to get to Rome.

This book is designed to get you to see that you are on the wrong train line, then put you on a train to Rome.

A Different View
of the World

So what was it that I saw that had such a profound impact on the way I relate to value, wealth and money?

Well, that is what the rest of this book is about. I will try to set you up for it though.

What I saw was that I had never really understood money — what it is or how it works.

I also saw that most of the people on the planet do not understand money — what it is or how it works.

Even though I grew up in a family that had a degree of financial success.

Even though I had a degree of financial success myself.

Even after 20 years in business.

It didn't matter.

The reality was I still didn't really understand how money worked and, more particularly, the relationship between value, money and wealth.

I couldn't. The context I was thinking from did not allow it.

I was looking at the world from a money-based view, and that made the world look a particular way.

A Money-Based View

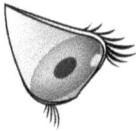

Most of us are used to living in a world where money exists as something of great importance. Our lives tend to be dictated by our pursuit of money. At a minimum, we have to be responsible for acquiring enough money for our basic needs and that of our family.

Placing a great importance on money is normal and, some would say, necessary in our society.

When we perceive something as being important, however, we give it a high level of attention. The high level of attention our society gives to money impacts how we view life.

This high level of importance our society places on money gives us a money-based view of the world.

Money-Based View

I'm not saying that a money-based view of the world isn't valid. However, a money-based view of the world is just a view. From this money-based view, the world looks a particular way.

Most of us are pretty familiar with how a money-based view of the world looks. Inside this view of the world, money seems very important and we give it a lot of attention. We have stock reports, conversations about low wages, courses on how to make more money, complaints about high taxes, government spending, interest rates, etc., etc.

There is a feel to a money-based view of the world. For most people, this money-based view feels oppressive, tight, controlled, and restrictive. Money is an entity which should be managed.

That is why many of us are working to become financially free — because we don't currently feel free. This comes more from the view we have of the world, however, than from the amount of money we actually have.

The strange thing is that when you look at the world from a money-based view, it does not give you an access to more wealth.

The access to wealth comes from somewhere else.

A Value-Based View

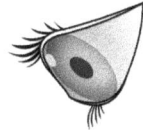

In this book, I want to give you a different view. I want to give you a value-based view of the world.

Value-Based View

Looking at the world from a value-based view will allow you to see yourself, others and the world of business completely differently.

It will give you a new depth in your relationship to wealth, value and money. It will give you a freedom that you have never experienced before, and a power that you will not have experienced before — no matter how much money you have.

It will also give you access to more money.

A value-based view of the world feels completely different.

There is a freedom. This is the view people are talking about when they say the world is abundant. A value-based view of the world feels free, creative and full of expression.

Having a value-based view of the world will exponentially increase your capacity to create wealth.

Money does not make the world go around. Value makes the world go around. Money just speeds up the journey.

PART 1
Wealth

Money

First, before we can fully explore wealth from a context of value, we have to do something else. We have to take money out of the equation.

I am not saying that money isn't important (it is important), or that I hate money (I don't – money is awesome).

It is just that I need to demolish your money-based view of the world so that you can see a new value-based view of the world. Don't worry, we will bring money back into the equation later on in a way that will give you more power with money than you ever had before.

So here we go. Let's get rid of some of the ideas that you currently hold about money.

1. First, stop trying to make money – you will never, ever make money.

Really. Here is the thing. Nobody makes money. It is a screwed up way of looking at the world. You will never, ever make money. The only people who make money work in the central bank. If you do make money, you will likely be put in jail for forgery. It is illegal.

Now, I know this seems obvious, but I want you to understand that we do not talk in these terms by accident. Most of us actually think in terms of trying to make money. It is an incredible waste of energy.

How much money do I make?

How can I make more money?

How can I make more money this year than I did last year?

How can I make more money than the person next door?

All that effort put into trying to do something which is actually impossible. I, myself, have sat down dozens of times and tried to work out how I can make more money. No wonder it was difficult to come up with a good answer.

This is one of the reasons people get so frustrated when it comes to wealth. It is a screwed up way of thinking.

You do not make money.

When you go to work and your boss pays you at the end of the month, you did not make money.

When your business does really, really well and you end up with $1 million more at the end of this year than you did at the end of last year, you did not make any money.

When you pull gold out of the ground at a cost of $800 an ounce and sell it for $1200 per ounce, you did not make money.

At any moment, there is a fixed amount of money in the world. You can increase your share of it, but that is very different from making it. I am not saying the amount of money in the world never changes — it can fluctuate according to government policy (more about this later). However, at any precise moment, the amount of money in the world is fixed. You can't make any more of it.

When you acquire money, you did not make it. Something else happened. That something else is what this book is about.

Stop trying to make money.

2. Money, itself, has no inherent value.

Most of us think of wealth in terms of money. Wealth is not money and money is not wealth.

Let me elaborate.

Here are two short questions:

Question 1

Your ship has been sunk in the Pacific Ocean and you have been washed up on a small island. You wake up and next to you is a large casket filled with $30 million in bank notes. You have no food, fresh water or companionship.

Are you wealthy?

Question 2

Your ship has been sunk in the Pacific Ocean and you have been washed up on a small island. You wake up and realise that a wild goat has been licking your face. You have no money. You can, however, hear the sound of running water. Next to you is a forest of fresh coconut trees, and standing below the trees is an abundance of naked humans of the sex to which you are most attracted.

Are you wealthy?

Money is not wealth. Money has no more value in this scenario than toilet paper.

3. Money is not wealth, it is only representative.

I want you to imagine that you go to bed tonight and, overnight, half the money on the planet disappears. Everyone who had two dollars now only has one dollar. Everyone who had two hundred British pounds now has only one hundred British pounds. Every single currency is reduced by half.

What is the impact on the planet? Has the wealth of the planet decreased?

No, it hasn't. There is absolutely no impact on the wealth of the planet. There may be some chaos while everyone tries to work out what happened but, theoretically, everyone could just half the price of everything and there would be no actual loss to society. There is absolutely no loss in value.

On the other hand…

Imagine you go to bed tonight and, overnight, half the oxygen on the planet disappears. What would be the impact?

Imagine you go to bed tonight and, overnight, half the drinking water on the planet disappears. What would be the impact?

Imagine you go to bed tonight and, overnight, half the food on the planet disappears. What would be the impact?

Imagine you go to bed tonight and, overnight, half the people on the planet disappear. What would be the impact?

Can you get the difference? Money is not wealth. Money just represents wealth. Money has a part to play in facilitating the transfer of wealth. Money itself, is not wealth.

The reason I am telling you all this is because you have to understand what money is not.

It is very likely that you have been giving money respect where it is not due.

There is, however, something that has much more power than we realise, and that deserves much more respect than we give it — that is *value.*

Again...

1. You will never, ever "make" money. Stop trying to make money. You are wasting your time and energy. Every time you even have a thought about making money, you are wasting energy.

2. Money, itself, has no inherent value. Money only has value in a marketplace which accepts it as currency. Stop thinking of value in terms of money.

3. Money is not wealth. Money is only representative of wealth. We will talk about this later in the book.

The main thing for the moment is... Money does not have the power that we often attribute it.

What does have power, however, is value.

Value

Okay, so what is the big fuss about value?

Why am I so interested in value, and why are so many people in the world interested in value?

Well, value *does* make the world go around.

First, let's talk about what value is.

Value is the usefulness of something. I personally define value as the capacity of an item or service to increase your experience of life.

In the world we live in, there are a great deal of products and services which have a usefulness to us. Their usefulness to us is their value.

If we had to value commodities in terms of usefulness, it would go something like this:

1. Oxygen
Without it we would be dead in 5 minutes.

2. Water
Without it we would be dead in 5 days.

3. Food
Without it we would be dead in 50 days.

4. Reproduction
Without it our species would be dead within 150 years.

There are other commodities that are essential for our survival, but you get the idea. These commodities have an incredible amount of value to us.

We also have other commodities which are not essential for life, but still hold value for us:

- good health
- companionship
- love
- music
- sport
- entertainment
- etc., etc.

Our world contains a whole bunch of resources which can increase our experience of life.

Each resource above has a value to us. It has a capacity to increase our experience of life.

Each of these commodities is a currency.

Currencies

Now, when I talk about currencies I am obviously not talking about the Australian Dollar, the US Dollar or the Chinese Yuan. When I talk about currencies, I mean any resource which you have available to you.

At any moment in time, you have a number of currencies that are available to you, and you will have a particular amount of that currency available to you.

You will have a certain amount of the currency of free time.

You will have a certain amount of the currency of health.

You will have a certain amount of the currency of energy.

You will have an amount of the currency of love.

You will have an amount of the currency of sexual energy.

You may have an amount of the currency of food.

You may have an amount of the currency of shelter.

You will have an amount in the currency of expertise.

Etc., etc.

All these items have value to you. They have a usefulness.

If you could add up the total quantity of the resources you have available to you, this would be your wealth.

Wealth

Definition of Wealth
> *1. An abundance of valuable possessions or money;*
> *2. A plentiful supply of a particular desirable thing.*
> **The above are the results of a Google search on "define wealth".**

Let's look at the definition of wealth.

Google's definition pretty much hits the mark; however, I personally define wealth as:

"An abundance of resources in the currencies that are important to you".

If we continue the conversation about currencies from the previous page, and if all currencies were measurable, we could, theoretically, create a chart of our current wealth.

A basic example would be:

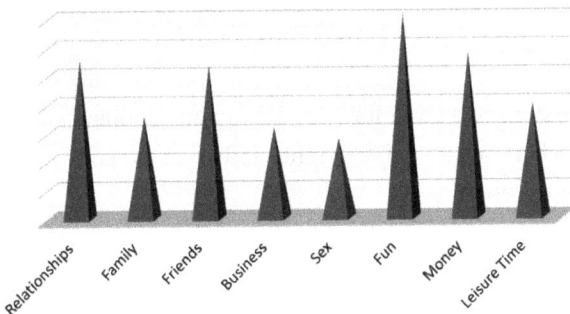

Imagine we can create a chart that completely represented a person's total wealth. Everyone would have their own chart and every chart would be different. Some people would have more love than others, some people would be better singers than others, some people would be better looking than others, and some people would have more free time than others.

Not only does everyone have their own level of each currency; people also have a different *ideal* level of each currency. People value each currency differently. One person may value sex more importantly than music. Another may value music more importantly than companionship. Another may value companionship more than sex.

Each person would have a chart of the actual amount of currency they have available in that area as well as a chart of the amount of currency they would like to have available in that area.
Here is an example:

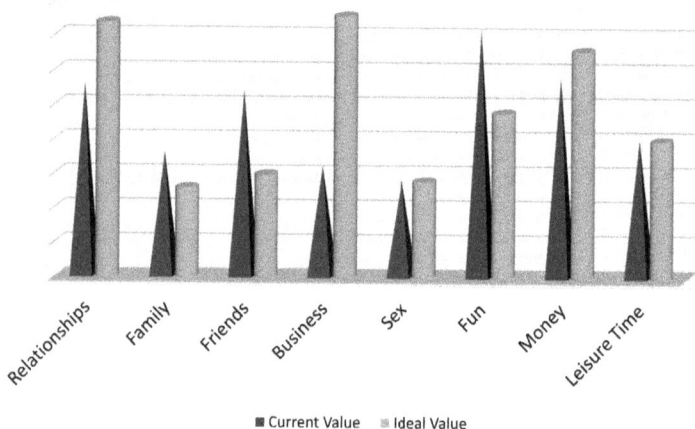

■ Current Value ▦ Ideal Value

If we created a chart for each person on the planet, each persons' "actual" chart would be different, and each persons' "ideal" chart would be different.

So how would we define wealth? Is it having lots of money? Is it having great relationships?

Ultimately, you will experience being wealthy when you have an abundance of resources in the areas that are important to you.

Your wealth is measured by how close your current chart of currencies is to your ideal chart of currencies. The beauty of this is that there is no fixed definition of wealth. It is all relative. It depends on what you personally value.

If we can create a chart to measure your current wealth and your ideal wealth, we can also then determine where the biggest gap is between your current and ideal wealth. Increasing the amount of the currency in those areas is what is going to create the biggest increase in wealth for you.

So, how do you increase your wealth in those areas?

How do you end up with an abundance of resources in the areas of life that are important to you?

Well, that is why we trade.

Trading

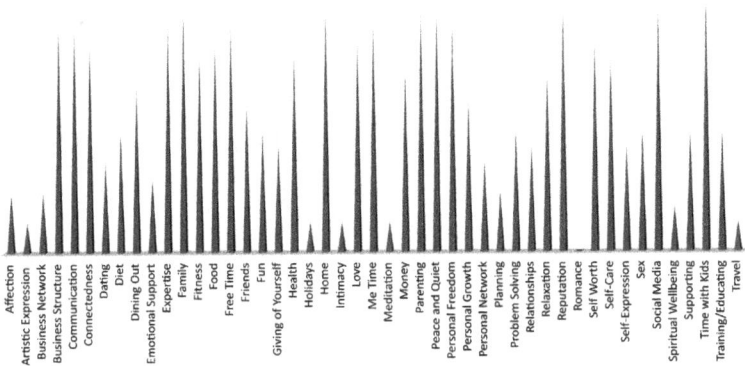

Affection | Artistic Expression | Business Network | Business Structure | Communication | Connectedness | Dating | Diet | Dining Out | Emotional Support | Expertise | Family | Fitness | Food | Free Time | Friends | Fun | Giving of Yourself | Health | Holidays | Home | Intimacy | Love | Me Time | Meditation | Money | Parenting | Peace and Quiet | Personal Freedom | Personal Growth | Personal Network | Planning | Problem Solving | Relationships | Relaxation | Reputation | Romance | Self Worth | Self-Care | Self-Expression | Sex | Social Media | Spiritual Wellbeing | Supporting | Time with Kids | Training/Educating | Travel

Trading Value

Every moment of every day, you are trading value. It is something you do subconsciously. All day long you trade value with others, and you trade value with yourself. You are trading value in every moment — you are doing it right now.

It is part of your design as a human being.

Simple examples of trades within a friendship:
When you call a friend on the phone, you could be:

> Trading "value as giving attention" for "value as feeling connected"

When you meet your friend to listen to their relationship issues, you could be:

> Trading "value as giving emotional support" for "value as feeling needed"

When you and your friend play a sport together, you could be:

> Trading "value as physical exertion" for "value as experiencing an adrenalin rush".

Simple examples of trades within a romantic relationship:
At dinner time, you may trade:

> "Value as doing the dishes" for "value as a cooked meal".

In a monogamous relationship, you may trade:

> "Value as not having sex with other partners" for "value as feeling secure in your relationship".

In a relationship where one partner has a job and the other is performing home duties, you may trade:

> "Value as financial support" (from the working partner) for "value as parenting support" (from the stay-at-home partner).

In families:
When your child falls over and scrapes their knee, you could be:

> Trading "value as empathy" for "value as not having to listen to your child cry".

When your child does their chores, they could be:

> Trading "value as physical work" for "value as appeasing the parent so they get fed".

When people in a family conform to the family's views, it could be:

> Trading "keeping quiet about your own views on life" for "value as feeling a part of the group".

With yourself:

When going to the gym, you may trade:

> "Value as exerting effort" for "value as feeling healthy and alert".

When eating fast food, you may trade:

> "Value as risk to health" for "value as high taste".

In the evening, you may trade:

> "Value as time watching television" for "value as not having to think about your day".

Every moment of every day you are trading value. The value will be in lots of different currencies, and often groups of currencies, but it is always value you are trading.

There are currencies being traded everywhere in your life, at every moment in your life.

The good news is, you do all of this naturally. You don't even have to think about it. What is more, you are designed to make choices that increase your wealth.

That is why you choose one resource over another. In every trade you make, you give something of lesser value to you, for something of more value to you. You pick that trade because you expect it to be more valuable than your other options.

That is why you have the friends you have.

That is why you have the partner you have.

That is why you have the life you have.

You are trading currencies all day long, and every moment is an attempt to increase your wealth given the resources you have at your disposal.

Making Conscious Trades

Given that you are trading value all day long in currencies you didn't even know you had, and you have been doing this subconsciously, imagine how much more effective you would be if you brought a level of consciousness to it.

Let's look more deeply at some of the trades you are in at this moment. Whilst reading this book, you are trading your time for some gain in currency, possibly:

* an expected increase in knowledge;
* a sense of freedom in the way you relate to money and wealth;
* a new relationship to wealth; or
* an access to having more money.

Reading this book is a trade. You may not be consciously making the trade, but you are making a trade, nonetheless.

You are making trades like this all day, every day.

What you put in your body.

Whether you exercise or not.

Whether you have lunch with this friend or that friend.

Every decision you make is a trade.

The trades we make are not haphazard, though. We make the trades we make because we expect those trades to give us the greatest perceived increase in value in currencies that are important to us.

To increase our wealth.

Every time we make a trade, we make it because we expect the trade to be profitable for us. We give something of less value for us, and we receive something of greater value for us.

For example, if you have five dollars and you buy a chicken sandwich for lunch, it is because, in that moment of hunger, the sandwich has more value to you than the five dollars or anything else you can buy in that moment with that five dollars. On another day, sushi may be more valuable to you than a chicken sandwich. That is why, on that day, you buy sushi for lunch.

We are constantly trading resources we perceive as less valuable for resources we perceive as being more valuable. We are attempting to get closer to our ideal range of currencies in order to increase our overall wealth.

Otherwise, we wouldn't be trading them.

This may be hard to get at first because you may look at some of the trades you are making and think, "Why am I making that trade?"

If you are making the trade, it is because, on some level, you perceive it as profitable for you. If you can't see why it is profitable, you have not yet distinguished the importance to you of the currency you are receiving.

Obsessions

Just because there is a "perceived" increase in value from the trade, however, doesn't mean there is a real increase in wealth. Most of us have our own obsessions that over-value particular currencies. We then tend to give more value out in order to gain that particular currency.

This can lead to people making terrible trades. People can become obsessed with exercise long past the point where it adds value to their life. People can become obsessed with a particular person to the point it becomes detrimental to their life. People can become obsessed with work to the point where it no longer creates value in their life.

In their extreme form, we call obsessions addictions. Addictions can cause people to make terrible trades. To an alcoholic, in the moment it may seem like a good trade to have a glass of wine, however, the trade would have immense negative impact on value in their life. An addict often makes decisions based on what feels good, without taking responsibility for the impact on the value in their life.

I smoked cigarettes from age 14 until the age of 21. I probably tried to stop smoking a few hundred times during this period, and it was a source of ongoing frustration for me. I knew that every time I put a cigarette in my mouth it reduced my wealth in the currencies of health, money and self-esteem. Most Monday mornings, I would commit to never having another cigarette. At some point, however, the pain of the craving would outweigh the perceived value of stopping smoking, and I would put another cigarette in my mouth. At 21, however, I became responsible for the impact on my life and, from then on, the trade no longer made sense. It was only a short matter of time before I stopped smoking completely.

Whether it be a normal trade, an obsession or an addiction, the more a person realises that every decision they make is a trade in value, the more power they will have in making decisions that increase their wealth.

The Importance Of Letting Go Of Wealth

One of the things that becomes apparent to me while working with clients to increase their wealth is that each client tends to put a lot of focus on one particular currency.

Strangely, it is usually a currency they already have a great deal of wealth in.

Often, early in life, a person decides that a currency is very important, and they focus on gaining wealth in this currency. It could be money, relationships, family, health, making a difference with others, etc.

After focussing on this currency for a number of years, however, they may have gained a great deal of value in this currency. The problem is that they still keep focussing on increasing this currency, even though gaining more value in this currency may create little increase and may even decrease their overall wealth.

Sometimes focussing on an area for too long can hold a person back from becoming wealthier.

It may be that the person's life is structured around holding on to the value in that area. If they were able to let go of some of their value in that area, or take their attention off holding on to the value in that area, it would allow more space for wealth.

Example

An example would be someone who works very hard. They may be lonely, single and have few friends, but have an abundance of money and professional esteem. Their life would probably be set up around keeping the currencies the same. The money that the person receives for working may have little positive impact on the person's real wealth. The time the person spends at work, and the health cost to them, may actually get in the way of them putting their attention on other areas which would increase their experience of life.

If you suggested to them to spend more time socialising, they would have to confront the possible loss of value in the area of money, and they would resist the change. What they would be resisting is giving up wealth in the area of money. People hate giving up value in any area. It is important to understand, however, that when you do this consciously, it can have an immeasurable impact on your life and your wealth.

In this scenario, taking some of the focus off the areas of money and career, and putting focus on generating good relationships, has the potential for much greater impact on the person's life. In addition, once the person's life is more balanced, they can then re-look at increasing their wealth in the original area. It is possible that after focussing on creating better relationships for a period, the benefit from the new increase in relationship skills would contribute to the person's ability to increase their financial wealth beyond what was previously possible.

Becoming Wealthier

There are two important things to understand if you are wanting to increase your wealth.

First, you need to connect to what is important to you. You have to understand the currencies you value the most.

Second, you have to master the distinctions of value. Fortunately, that is what Part 2 of this book is about.

You are heading in the right direction.

PART 2
Value

Mastering the distinctions of value are at the heart of what it takes to create wealth, and there are three essential components to mastering value:

- Becoming value aware;
- Becoming great at creating value; and
- Capturing value.

Let's discuss each in turn.

Value Awareness

Becoming Aware Of Value

The first step in mastering a value-based lifestyle is to become *aware* of value.

When people hear the word "value", they tend to think it means getting a lot for their money.

That is not what I mean when I talk about becoming aware of value. As we have discussed, value is the usefulness of something — the ability of a product or service to improve your experience of life.

If you want to be great at trading, it makes sense to become very conscious of the value of what you are trading.

You are trading value all day long and every trade impacts your wealth. Even if you only marginally increased your awareness of trading value, it would have a massive impact across your whole life.

Because we grow up in such a money centric world, we have an incredibly low conscious awareness of value. When we grow up in a money centric environment, we tend to judge everything in financial terms. It seems like anything that leaves us with more money is a good thing. Anything that leaves us with less money, not so good.

More About Money

It makes sense how this happened. We all like to be able to measure and quantify things. It seems to make things easier. Measuring value in financial terms gives us the experience that value is measurable and quantifiable. Measuring value in financial terms also gives us an experience of progress. We can put metrics to it. Assign it a number. Increase the number then feel good because we believe we have made progress.

However, just because I put a number to the value of an item, it doesn't mean that the number reflects the item's true value. Also, just because the rest of the world thinks of value in financial terms, it doesn't mean that thinking in financial terms works.

One of the reasons it doesn't work is because, once you give something a financial price tag, people think that price tag reflects the item's true value. Items that have a larger dollar number to them are perceived to have more value than items that have a lower number. In actuality, it doesn't mean the item has more value to you.

Also, all over the world there are:

- people who are sacrificing their health to try to get more money. This is not a good trade.
- people who are not having kids because they hear kids are too expensive (not smart – if you want more kids, have more kids. If you don't, don't. The money aspect is not nearly as important as you think).

There are some things that cannot be measured in financial terms: personal freedom, self-expression, presence, self-awareness or connected relationships.

The world currently greatly overvalues money as a resource. As we have said numerous times in the previous pages, money is not wealth; money represents wealth.

The biggest problem I have with people thinking of the world in money centric terms is that it takes their attention away from thinking in terms of value – the actual value in terms of a product's ability to improve their experience of life.

There is so much energy and attention wasted in conversations about money that have little impact on a person's wealth.

How much money do I earn?

How much money do they earn?

How can I earn more money?

How much debt do I have?

How much does property cost?

Looking at money in this way is detrimental. You place your attention on money, when doing so is not going to make a difference. Paradoxically, if you place your attention on value, you will actually end up with more money.

The amount of attention most people give to money, and the importance that money is given in our lives, is disproportionately large compared to the impact it has on our life. Society has come to a point where people see money as the aim when money is, in actual fact, never the aim. The aim is always something else.

When people are starving, it is not because they don't have any money. It is because they don't have any food.

When people are homeless, it is not because they don't have any money. It is because they don't have a safe place to sleep.

When you want a massage and can't get one, it is not because you don't have any money. It is because you don't have anyone to give you a massage.

It is never *ever* about the money.

When people think in terms of money, it is very lazy thinking. Over time, this lazy thinking lessens their awareness of value. People become removed from value. They stop thinking through transactions and become less aware of the value of what is being traded. This lack of awareness is detrimental to their wealth. When people are not aware of value, they can make terrible trades and it can have an unnecessary impact on themselves, their friends and families, their communities and on the world.

To become truly wealthy in any currency, yes even to acquire more money – you need to start developing your capacity to see the world in terms of value.

At first, it will take some effort on your part. I recommend starting with one area of life that you would like to impact. Take a few minutes to write down some of the trades you are making in your life.

You will likely find it difficult at first because we are not trained to look at the world this way.

Exercise

We have talked a little about what value is and how you are trading value all day long. To really capitalize on this conversation, however, you need to be able to become aware of value in real time. You need to be proactive in looking at some aspects of your life, and a good way to practice this is to sit down and write out the trades you are making.

When writing out transactions I recommend using the following language:

I traded "value as" for "value as"

E.g.

I traded "value as money" for "value as chicken sandwich".

I traded "value as a smile" for "value as a date".

I traded "value as doing the dishes" for "value as a peaceful night with my partner".

Wording the trade in this way helps us train our minds back to thinking in terms of value, rather than just thinking in terms of the commodity.

I want to stress that it is not important what you write down. What is important is doing the exercise. The thinking in itself will expand your awareness of value, and you will begin to see value being traded of which you were not previously conscious. You may find your brain struggling to think this way at first. This is normal. Keep doing the exercise and it will get easier.

Taking time to look at your life in this way will be incredibly valuable. I recommend each day writing out at least three trades you made. Do this exercise every day for a month.

Trading Multiple Currencies

As you become more aware of trading value in your life, you will realise that you are often not trading "value in one currency" for "value in another currency". You are often trading "multiple currencies" for "multiple currencies".

Trading Time for Money

One of the conversations I have often heard is that, "People in traditional jobs trade time for money".

This is incorrect. No one trades their time for money. No one needs your time. If you went to work tomorrow and sat on the office floor for eight hours, you would likely be fired.

Your boss does not need your time. Your boss hires you for other currencies that you bring.

A slightly more elaborate version of the trade would look like this:

Value as	Traded For	Value as
-Expertise -Experience -Contacts -Manpower	⇔	-Training -Self-esteem -Social Interaction -Money

If you think that you are being paid for your time, you are disconnected from the actual trade that is being made.

If your boss is paying you $50,000 or $100,000 or $500,000 per annum, it is because your services to the company are worth a lot more than that. Otherwise, it wouldn't make sense to employ you. If you want to capitalise on your worth, no matter what currency you are trading, you need to understand where the value lies in what you are providing.

Romantic Relationships

Relationships are another great example of trading "multiple currencies" for "multiple currencies".

Here is a very basic example of multiple currencies that could be traded in a romantic relationship:

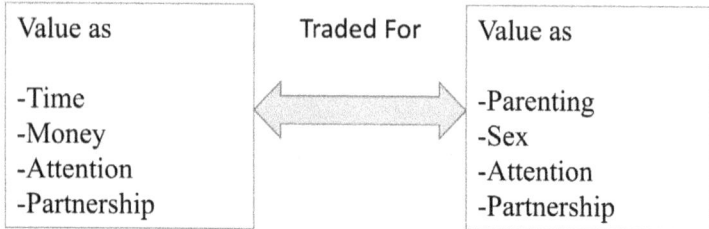

Value as	Traded For	Value as
-Time -Money -Attention -Partnership	⟵⟶	-Parenting -Sex -Attention -Partnership

Of course, romantic relationships are more complex than this. There are many different currencies being traded, desired, and sometimes even demanded. That is what makes relationships so difficult.

However, being unclear *why* romantic relationships are so difficult makes it even worse. You may feel the pressure of your desire for a particular currency, or your partner's desire for a particular currency, but not understand what is going on. This leads to more and more pressure, which is often detrimental to the relationship.

The clearer you become on your desires:

1. The easier they are to communicate;
2. The more chance of having your desires met; and
3. The more chance of a fulfilling relationship.

Value is Dynamic

As you become more and more aware of value, one of the things you will realise is that value is also not fixed. Value is dynamic. It is changing moment by moment. Different people value different things, and even the same person will place different value on things under different circumstances and at different periods of life.

One day you may be walking through a city and be offered a

bottle of water for free and you refuse because you are not thirsty. Another day you may be stranded in a desert and would happily trade everything you own for the same bottle of water.

Human beings change, as do our needs.

What is important to you now may not be what is important to you in one day, one year, five years or ten years.

The *value* of a commodity is never fixed.

Your ability to be aware of the changing nature of value is one of the greatest skills you can develop. It may seem like a lot of work to keep assessing the value of things. However, you already have this skill. You are naturally re-assessing the value of things to you all day long. You may just not be aware that you are doing this.

Following the Value

A few years ago, when I was in my last business, my chart probably looked like this:

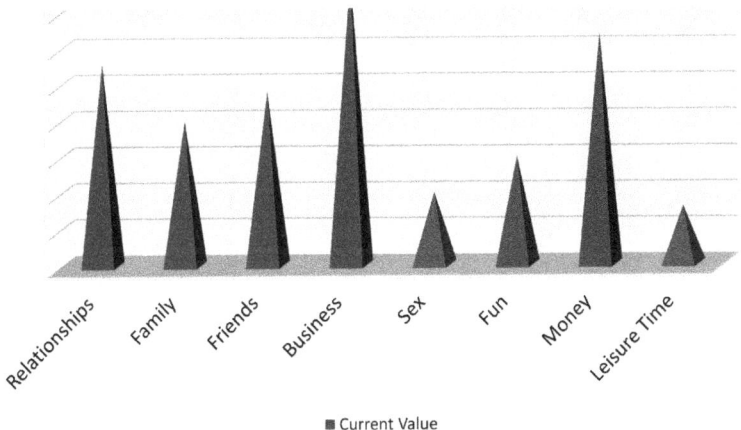

■ Current Value

At this time, the chart would have been close to my ideal wealth in each of these areas.

When my first son became four, however, I started to realise that in one year he would be at school. I also became aware that unless I altered my lifestyle, I would miss a valuable opportunity to connect with him at this period of his life.

My priorities had shifted. My ideal values began to look more like this:

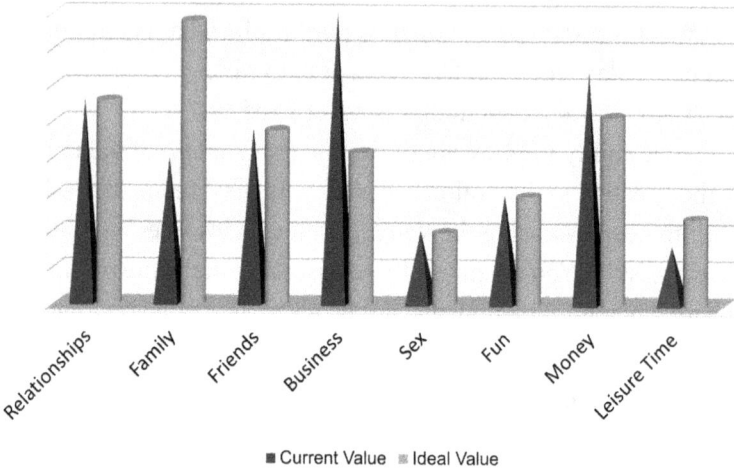

■ Current Value ▦ Ideal Value

I decided to sell my business to take a year off, which contributed to my chart becoming more like this:

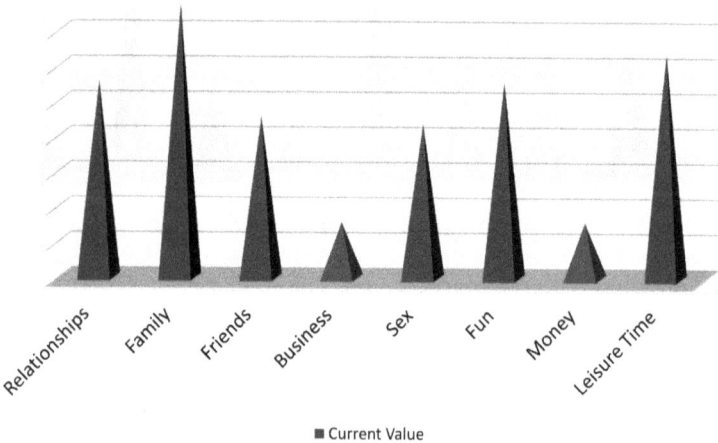

■ Current Value

During this period, although I was worse off in financial terms, my quality of life was great. I experienced being wealthier during this period than in many other periods of my life. I had a great deal of quality time with my children, I worked on my personal relationships and my relationship with myself. I also had a great deal of time to plan what was next for me in my business life.

After spending three years off, however, my priorities were again different. I wanted to contribute to the world on a larger scale.

My ideal chart now looked like this:

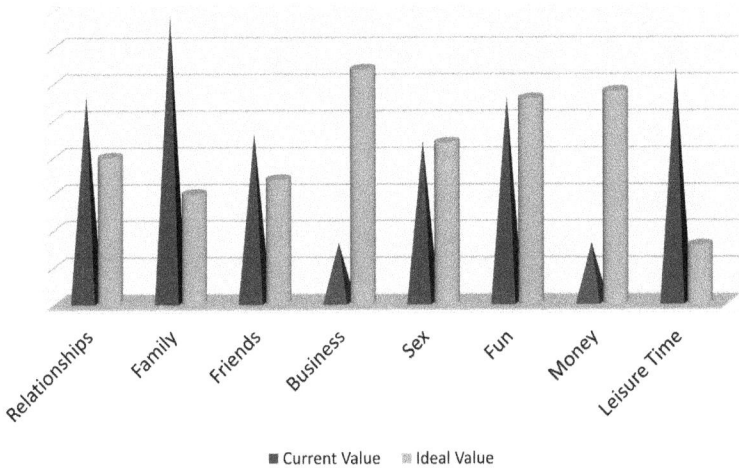

■ Current Value　▩ Ideal Value

I altered my focus and started building a new business.

Understanding that your ideal wealth changes, and allowing yourself to adjust your life to your changing needs, is one of the most valuable gifts you can give yourself.

We are not fixed beings. Adjusting your life according to what you value in a particular period of your life is an important part of managing your experience of wealth.

The Value of Value Awareness

As you become more value aware, you will start to see things in your life that you didn't previously notice. You will begin to be more aware of what you are doing in your life, why you are doing it and also who you are doing it with.

More importantly, however, you will start to notice where value is being created.

The fact that value can be created is one of the most important aspects of value, and it is central to your capacity to create wealth.

It is also the primary reason I wrote this book.

Let's learn about creating value.

Value Creation

Creating value is one of the most driving and enlivening aspects of my life. I love the experience of creating value. When I first saw that all through my life I had been creating value without realising it, my experience of life altered.

This is one of the main reasons why living from a value-based context is so valuable. As beings, we all want to experience being someone who is valuable. The times we experience this the most, however, are when we notice ourselves having a positive impact on others.

When you are looking at the world from a money-based view, it is much harder to see the positive impact you are having in the world. You tend to just see the money and, as we have said, money can never be created.

You can, however, create value. You have been creating value your whole life, you just haven't been aware of it. Because you have not been aware of it, you have not been able to be responsible for the value you have been creating. The more you experience – and are aware of – your capacity to create value, the more value you will create.

Bill & Ben

Let me tell you the story of Bill and Ben.

Bill and Ben are two farmers. Bill has a grain farm, and each week he makes ten loaves of bread. Ben has a dairy farm, and each week he makes ten pats of butter. They live close to each other, and every Saturday morning they meet up to trade.

Each week Bill swaps Ben two loaves of bread for two pats of butter.

Now, I want you to think about this transaction from the point of view of value (usefulness).

Before the trade, Bill has ten loaves of bread. After the trade, he has eight loaves of bread and two pats of butter.

Is he better off after the trade? Yes – the two pats of butter he gained are more useful to him than the two loaves of bread he gave away.

He now has butter to put on his toast each morning. He also still has bread to make the toast.

Also, before the trade, Ben has ten pats of butter. After the trade he has eight pats of butter and two loaves of bread.

Is he better off after the trade? Yes – the two loaves of bread he gained are more useful to him than the two pats of butter he gave away.

He now has bread for toast each morning. He also still has butter left to put on his toast.

Both people are better off in terms of value after the trade than before the trade.

Why is this?

Diminishing Usefulness

Generally, the more the quantity you have of an item, the less useful each unit of that item will be to you. Even to one person at a particular time, the value of an item can change depending on how much they have of it.

Think about this.

If Bill makes ten loaves of bread a week, each loaf of bread has a different value to him.

The first loaf is very useful. It may stop him from starving to death.

Though not quite so valuable as the first, the second loaf is still very useful. It will keep away pangs of hunger.

The third loaf, again, is slightly less useful, although it still has value. It means he can have extra food when he is hungry.

By the time you look at the tenth loaf of bread, the usefulness to Bill's life is fairly negligible. Three loaves of bread is all he needs a week. Whether he makes ten loaves or nine loaves will make no real difference to his life.

Let's give an arbitrary measure to the usefulness of each loaf and say the first loaf has a usefulness of 10, the second a usefulness of 9, the third a usefulness of 8, etc., all the way to the last, which has a usefulness of 1.

Let's draw a graph of the usefulness of each loaf of bread.

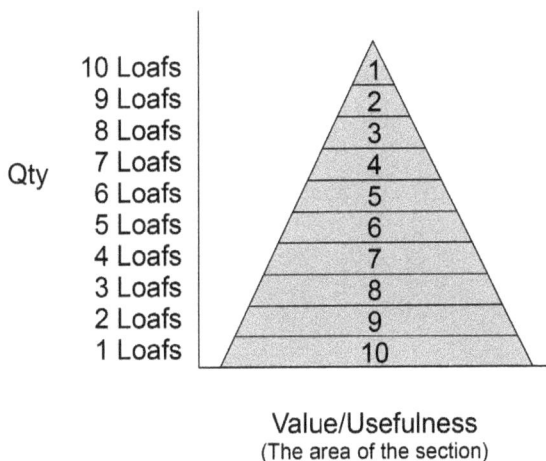

Qty	
10 Loafs	1
9 Loafs	2
8 Loafs	3
7 Loafs	4
6 Loafs	5
5 Loafs	6
4 Loafs	7
3 Loafs	8
2 Loafs	9
1 Loafs	10

Value/Usefulness
(The area of the section)

If we were to measure Bill's wealth of bread in terms of usefulness, he would have a total wealth of 55 (the total area of the triangle).

$$10+9+8+7+6+5+4+3+2+1=55.$$

Total Usefulness = 55

Qty	
10 Loafs	1
9 Loafs	2
8 Loafs	3
7 Loafs	4
6 Loafs	5
5 Loafs	6
4 Loafs	7
3 Loafs	8
2 Loafs	9
1 Loafs	10

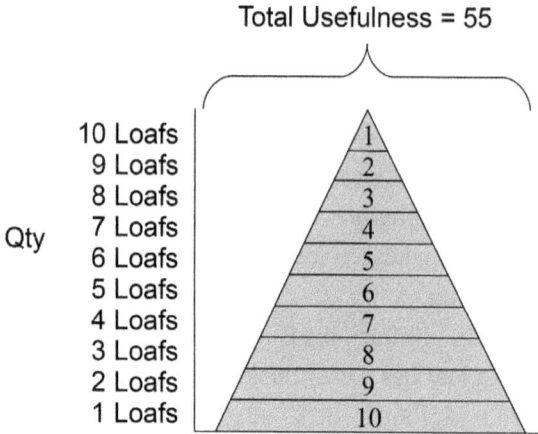

We can do the same for Ben's wealth in butter.

The first pat of butter has a usefulness of 10, the second a usefulness of 9, the third a usefulness of 8, etc., all the way to the last, which has a usefulness of 1.

Ben's wealth of butter in terms of usefulness, we could also say, is 55.

$$10+9+8+7+6+5+4+3+2+1=55.$$

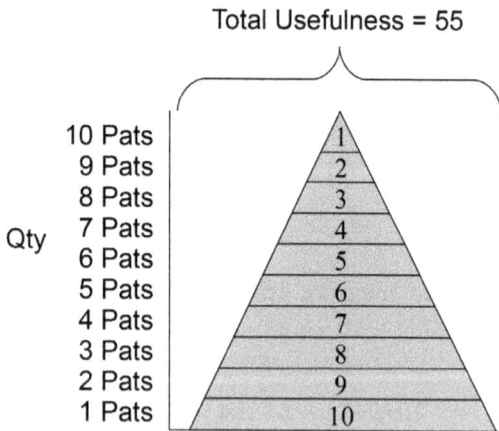

Total Usefulness = 55

Qty	
10 Pats	1
9 Pats	2
8 Pats	3
7 Pats	4
6 Pats	5
5 Pats	6
4 Pats	7
3 Pats	8
2 Pats	9
1 Pats	10

If we added together their wealth in terms of usefulness, we would have 55 for Ben and 55 for Bill, giving a wealth of 110.

We could then say our small, two-person economy has a usefulness of 110.

Total Usefulness = 110

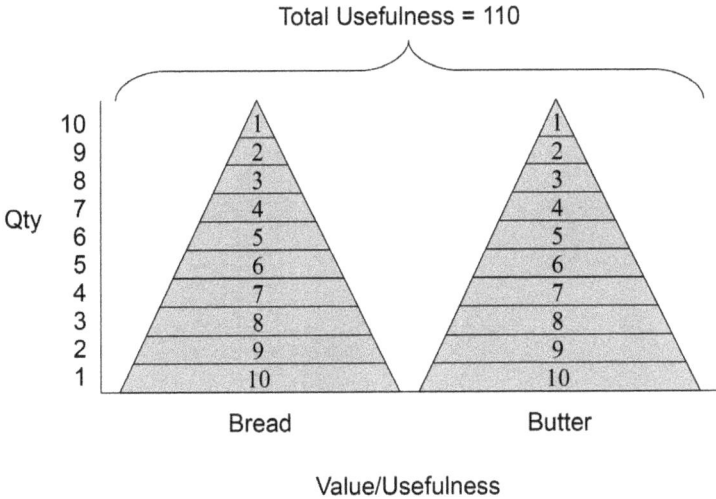

Value/Usefulness

How Value Is Created

Now let's look at this again after Bill gives Ben the bread, but before Bill receives the butter from Ben.

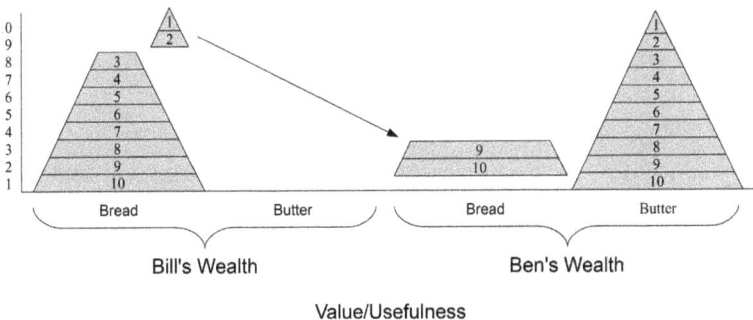

Value/Usefulness

Note that although the ninth and tenth loaves of bread for Bill had a low usefulness (of 1 and 2), when he gives the bread to Bill, it has a high usefulness (of 10 and 9) because Ben doesn't have any other bread.

The same happens when Ben gives his butter to Bill. What had a low usefulness (because Ben has lots of butter) now has a high usefulness (because Bill has no other butter).

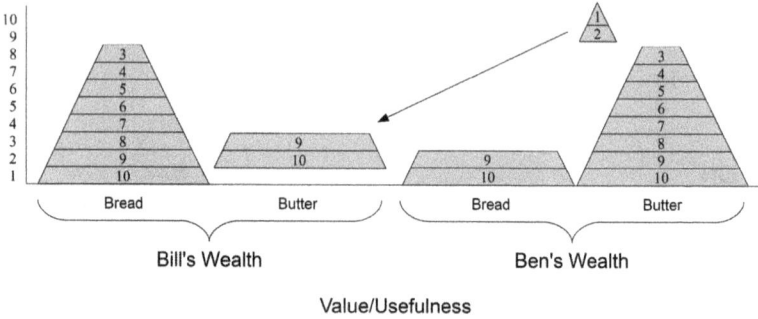

Value/Usefulness

The wealth of Bill and Ben in terms of usefulness now looks like this.

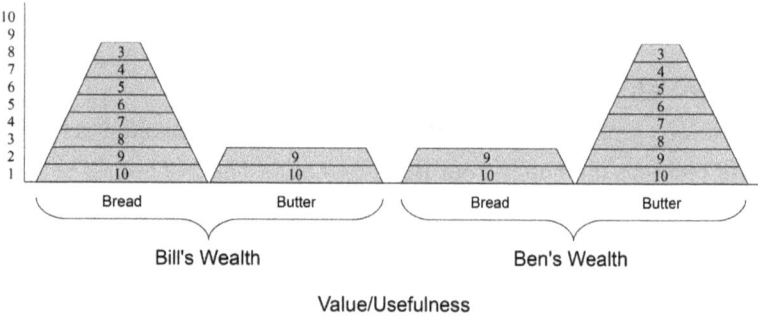

Value/Usefulness

If we add up the total usefulness of Bill's bread and butter, it now comes to 71.

52 from Bread (10+9+8+7+6+5+4+3)

19 from Butter (9+10)

If we add up the total usefulness of Ben's bread and butter, it also now comes to 71.

19 from Bread (9+10)

52 from Butter (10+9+8+7+6+5+4+3)

The total value of our little two-person economy now comes to 142.

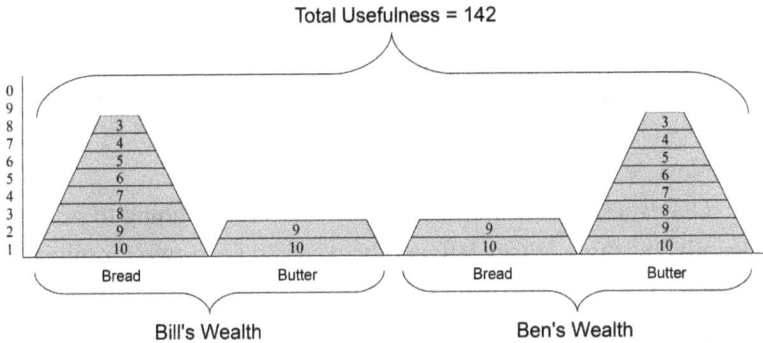

Total Usefulness = 142

Bill's Wealth

Ben's Wealth

Given the total value of the economy prior to trading was 110, we have increased the wealth of the total economy by 32.

Each individual party's previous wealth was 55 and now is 71. Each party had a personal net increase in wealth of 16. Both parties are better off. In this trade, value was *created*.

How can this be when no new resources or skills were brought into our economy?

Well, trading creates value. When two people trade, they are each giving something of less value to themselves and receiving something of more value.

The main thing to get out of this exercise is that almost every time two people make a trade, there is an increase in usefulness for both parties. When two people trade, it creates a net increase in wealth.

This is why people trade all day long. When two people trade, it is likely that both people are better off. Why else would they make the trade?

When you look at the world from the context of value, there is not a winner and a loser. Both parties win.

This is particularly important to understand if you are a business person.

Money

Now, I have a question to ask you. Did the purpose of this transaction have anything to do with money?

No. It's pretty simple, right? None of this trade had anything to do with money. It was all about value. People traded because the item they gained had more usefulness than the item they traded. Money didn't even come into it.

Now, let's look at this scenario again:

One week, Bill has been sick and his bread is going to be late. He only has three loaves left, and he wants to keep two for himself. He does, however, still want two pats of butter.

He offers to give Ben one loaf of bread now and to write him a promissory note (which can be redeemed at a later date) for the other loaf in return for his normal two pats of butter.

Three days later, Bill has more bread. He calls Ben, who comes over, provides the promissory note, and picks up the bread.

The transaction is the same as before, but part of the transaction was postponed.

Now let's ask the question again — did the purpose of this transaction have anything to do with money?

The answer is still no. None of this trade had anything to do with money. It was still all about value. People traded because the other item had more usefulness than the item they traded.

Money (which was the promissory note) only came in as a tool to facilitate the transaction. The purpose of the trade was still to increase value.

This is what money is — a tool to facilitate trade. This is what is happening all over the world when people use money. The transactions are never about the money. You are always trading for value. It just looks like it is about money because you normally only think about the transaction from your side. You see yourself hand over $5 and receive a chicken sandwich and think that the transaction has something to do with money. If you had followed the $5 note through the transactions for the ten years before or the ten years after, you would realise that the money was not the important aspect of the trade. What was important was that through trading, value was created along the way.

Stored Value

This brings us to one of the awesome qualities about money.

Money is a great way of storing value. It allows me to provide a service for someone and, instead of them providing value in return, they can give me a promissory note (money) that can be redeemed later in another store.

It is a way of storing value. I provide the service. I don't need value back from the client in the form of a service immediately, so he provides me with money instead.

The value is stored in the money until I head down the street and use it to buy myself a chicken sandwich, at which point the stored value is released. It is then stored value for the sandwich shop owner, who may release it through giving it to his staff as wages for their service. The staff then have it as stored value which they then release by paying the rent on their home, etc., etc.

The point is that trading is never actually to do with money. It is always to do with value. Sometimes you may trade for a currency you will use right now. Other times you may trade for a currency you can use later (stored value – usually in the form of money).

Money makes it easier for us to trade with each other. The easier it is for each other to trade, the more we will trade and the more we trade, the more value gets created.

It is not about the money, though. It just looks that way because we only see one side of the transaction – selling an item or buying an item.

Money is a tool. Society created a tool called "value as money", which helps to facilitate trading.

Most of us have just gotten used to thinking of wealth in terms of money, but it is incorrect.

As I said before, money is not wealth. Money facilitates wealth.

Destroying Value

Value can be created, but can value be destroyed? Yes, it can.

Bill could have eight loaves of bread and two pats of butter.

Ben could have eight pats of butter and two loaves of bread.

Then Bill could trade his two pats of butter (which have more value for him) for two loaves of bread (which have less value for him). Ben would then receive two pats of butter (which would have less value for him) in exchange for two loaves of bread (which have more value for him).

Each person would be worse off after the trade than they were before they traded. Value was lost.

The wealth of both parties decreased and the wealth of our two-person economy decreased.

It wouldn't be smart to make this trade, but people make trades like this all the time; eating foods that are not good for them, watching television, playing video games, being in relationships that are toxic and working in jobs they don't want to be in.

People with addictions are also making terrible trades. It is not the alcohol, drugs, porn, or work that are the problem. It is whether they are having a positive effect in increasing their wealth.

That is when an activity becomes an addiction. When it is becoming detrimental to your life.

There are trades made every day that will diminish value. Mostly it is because people are not aware of value and not responsible for the trades they're making, and some people don't understand the whole distinction of value being created and value being diminished or destroyed.

Most people make trades based on their programming or neuroses. The neuroses may be getting some payoff from the trade, but it is not creating value. Starting to think in terms of value can have all sorts of benefits for your life. When you become aware of value, you'll notice that some of the trades aren't working for you, and they may not be working for others.

Becoming A Master Of Creating Value
Your ability to create value is the greatest factor in dictating your level of wealth. In fact, if you look at anyone who has a great deal of

wealth in a particular currency, they will be great at creating value in that currency. Some people work hard at it. Some people do it easily.

It doesn't matter. Whether you are creating value or not is what is important.

Having a great relationship comes from creating value for, and with, your partner.

Being a great parent comes from creating value for, and with, your kids.

Being a great business person comes from creating value for, and with, your shareholders, staff, and customers.

If you want to be wealthy, you have to become someone who is masterful at creating value. When you start to create value in a particular currency, there is more of that currency available for everyone.

Just being great at creating value in itself, however, is not enough. You also need to be able to capture an appropriate portion of the value you are creating.

Value Capture

There is a third step to mastering the distinctions of value. You need to capture a portion of the value you create.

It is possible for value to be captured in any currency. However, in our daily lives, we will often think of this in financial terms.

Capturing value is what most people think of as "making money". It is the part that has you end up with more money than you started with. We will go into how this works in a later chapter.

If you are creating value, it makes sense for you to capture a portion of the value you create. In fact, when you create value, you have an obligation to capture a portion of that value for yourself.

Why do I say an obligation?

Well, the people who you trade with also benefit from trading with you. If you are not capturing a large enough portion of the value you are creating, then you are going to go bankrupt. Everyone has overheads, even if it is just food and shelter. You have an obligation to other people to maintain your ability to keep trading so that they can continue to create value with you.

If you can no longer trade, the people you trade with will be worse off. Therefore, you have an obligation to them to maintain your capacity to trade.

This is the same whether it be a corporate entity or a personal relationship.

Bank

Let's take a bank. I have deliberately chosen a bank, as banks are often seen as the least value-producing business entities. I could, however, have chosen any business.

Whether you like it or not, banks create value. It has more value for me to place my money into a bank's hands than to keep it under the mattress. Under the mattress, I would be concerned that it would be stolen, my house would go up in flames or I would forget where I had put it. It is worth me paying $5 per month for bank fees.

On top of that, I can pay bills online, swipe my card at a checkout, check my balance in an instant and transfer between different accounts – both mine and others'.

Let's look at this transaction:

A customer pays $5 to the bank, which is "value as money". In return, she receives monthly "value as bank services".

The bank provides "value as bank services"		The customer provides "value as money"

Let's look at where value is created in this transaction. We will measure the value that is created in terms of value as money.

For the bank, the service is provided at a cost to the bank of $3 per month.

What is the value that is received by me as a customer? Is it $5 per month? No. It has to be more than that, otherwise there would be no point in me doing the trade.

So what is the value to me? How much would I pay before it was no longer worth me putting my money in a bank?

Would I pay $50? $100?

Let's say the actual value to me is worth $50 per month. Any more and I would store my money in a mattress.

Then the value that has been created in the transaction is $47.

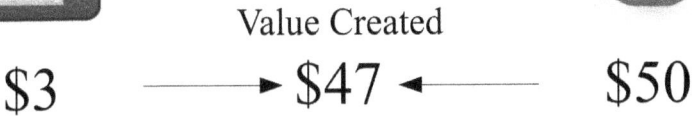

Value Created

$3 ⟶ $47 ⟵ $50

So how is the value split?

Well, the bank captures $2 worth of the value created ($5 charged – $3 costs).

The customer captures $45 worth of the value created ($50 in benefit – $5 costs).

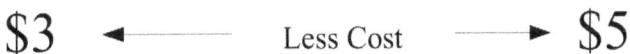

$5 ⟵ Value Received ⟶ $50

$3 ⟵ Less Cost ⟶ $5

You could say that the benefit to the client is not real, however, this is not true. The benefit is the time and energy that the client saves by not needing to check her mattress every night, by not needing to walk to the post office to pay her bills or by not needing to visit her friend to pay back the money she borrowed.

All this value created for the client allows her to spend more time and energy on other value-creating activities elsewhere. Both parties getting together creates value, and both parties capture value.

Here you have the makings of a good long-term relationship in which both parties are wealthier after the transaction.

Unsustainable Trading

In the transaction above, it is possible that the same total value is created, however, only one of the parties captures value.

The bank could lower its price to $2. The value captured for the bank would be -$1 per month. The value captured for the customer would be $48.

$2	◄——— Value Received ———►	$50
$3	◄——— Less Cost ———►	$2
$-1	◄——— Value Captured ———►	$48

Obviously, for the bank, this transaction does not make sense. The bank is not capturing enough value to sustain the relationship. This is, however, also a problem for the customer. If the bank is not capturing enough value, it will go out of business. This would be a major problem for the customer. They would then either have to start storing their money under the mattress (in which case, they would lose a great deal of value each month) or find another bank. Even finding another bank would cost them value. It would be a major exercise to set up accounts again, internet banking, payees, etc.

It is in our interest to ensure the people we trade with are capturing enough of the value to keep trading. It is not in your interest for them to go out of business.

The same exercise could be done from the bank's side.

If the bank charged $51 for their services, they would no longer have the client's business. It would no longer be a profitable trade. The client would place their funds under the mattress. The bank would then lose out on the opportunity to create value with the client and the resulting $2 per month of value that could be captured.

As a business person, you have an obligation to ensure that the people you are doing business with are capturing enough value from the transaction. If not, that customer has a limited life span with you. This relationship is unsustainable. It is not good business.

What is often not grasped is that when a business goes into liquidation, the clients of the business are often the ones who are most impacted, even if they are not directly impacted by financial loss during the liquidation.

In this banking example, the client benefits by $45 every month by trading with the bank. The bank benefits by $2. If the banks all went out of business, who would be worse off going forward?

The Purpose Of A Business

As a business owner, you are responsible for the business making a profit.

Let's get one thing clear however:

The purpose of a business is not to make money.

The purpose of a business is not even to create value so that you can make money.

The purpose of a business is to create value, and one of the things to be responsible for is making a profit so that you can continue to create value. It is very important to understand this.

The purpose of a business is to amplify the stakeholder's capacity to create value.

A business allows us to create value more efficiently than we would without the business.

Let's look at this a bit more closely.

The value you create by being in business includes all stakeholders, as follows:

Your shareholders: By creating value, you continue to capture some of that value and make a profit so that you can distribute a portion of that value as dividends (value as money) to your shareholders.

Your staff: By creating value, and then capturing a portion of that value, you can distribute a portion of that value to staff as wages (value as money).

Your suppliers: Your suppliers create and capture value from trading with you (value as money), otherwise they would not be in business.

Your customers: Your customers buy from you for a reason. Whatever they get in value from purchasing from you, it provides value for them. If it wasn't a profitable transaction in a currency that was important to them, they would not buy from you.

The general public: When you create value for your shareholders, staff, suppliers and customers, these stakeholders end up wealthier in many different currencies and, therefore, have more resources to then provide for the people in their life. This filters out to the public at large.

You may think you have a responsibility to make a profit so that you can live your dream life. The great thing is that, in doing so, you will provide value for the rest of the world, too.

Entrepreneurship

By now you will hopefully realise that business is not about making money. It is all about creating value.

Business is about creating value, and entrepreneurship is about creating value.

A business is an entity that brings together a number of resources to increase the value that can be created from those resources. Imagine I want to set up an I.T. company. I take on a small I.T. project. It is the first time I have delivered this project, but I am sure I can provide value.

The value of the completed project to the client is $50,000. I charge the client $25,000.

The job costs me $15,000 to complete.

I make $10,000 profit. The client makes $25,000 profit.

Here we have the makings of a good business.

Let's look at the outcome of this transaction.

The project is a value positive transaction for the client. He is better off after the project is complete.

The project is a value positive transaction for me. I am better off after the project is complete.

Our ability to create value for each other is the basis of our relationship. Without the client, I have no one to create value for. Without me, the client has no way of completing the project.

The ability to see scenarios where value can be created is at the heart of entrepreneurship.

Whether you:

- Create value by taking iron ore from the ground where it has little usefulness and turning it into iron, which has a lot of usefulness.

- Take your personal energy and physicality and provide someone who is stressed and has little energy with a massage.
- Take your building experience and build someone a house.

In essence, this is what an entrepreneur does. He looks for opportunities where he can create value.

A great tool to *help* him to create value is money.

PART 3
Money

Money

So far, we have been talking a lot about value and very little about money, because understanding value is what is going to impact your experience of wealth.

Let's look again at money, though.

What is Money

As we discussed earlier, money has no inherent value. It only has value in a marketplace that recognises it as currency.

If money has no inherent value, why do people put so much attention on it? Why does it seem so powerful?

Well, there are qualities to money that allow for an immensely positive impact to society.

Traditionally, money is said to have three main uses:

1. A store of value;
2. A medium of exchange; and
3. A unit of account.

I'm not going to go through each of these uses in this book in great detail. These uses can be looked up on Google, or read in any economics book.

I will, however, touch on some interesting properties that I find incredibly useful in my dealings.

A Store of Value

As discussed earlier, whenever you provide a product or service for a customer, you are providing them value as fish, eggs, bread, butter, massage – whatever the product or service is. In return, the customer may then give you the equivalent value as money. As we have discussed, money itself has no value to you. The value is stored to be released at a time that suits you. You can then take the money to a marketplace that accepts the money as currency and release that value by purchasing, for example, a chicken sandwich when you are hungry, which does have value.

Money is a great way to store value. This quality is not exclusive to money, however. This would be the same for any non-depreciating asset. Traditionally, metals were used as money because they could be easily fashioned into coins and jewellery, and they didn't tarnish over time. Paper money then became more widely used as it was much easier to carry. Nowadays, even paper money is becoming superseded by bank cards, which are even more convenient.

In all these examples, however, money is a way of temporarily storing value.

The Relationship Between Money And Value

There was a time when money was a literal replacement for value. It was a replacement for gold. This was described as the gold standard. Money would represent the gold that was held in the vaults of the banks that printed the bank notes.

During the 20th century, however, the money systems of countries changed and, since then, currency has been known as Fiat money. Fiat money is not connected to any metal standard. In reality, however, modern day currency is connected to value. Contrary to what some believe, governments cannot just print money without it impacting the economy. The amount of money has to be related to the value of goods and services in the economy.

To understand how this works, you need to imagine there are two pools. You have one pool holding all the money, and another pool holding the products and services.

To keep things simple. Let's say our whole economy consists of four light bulbs, and the total amount of money in the economy is $4. Each light bulb would, therefore, be worth $1.

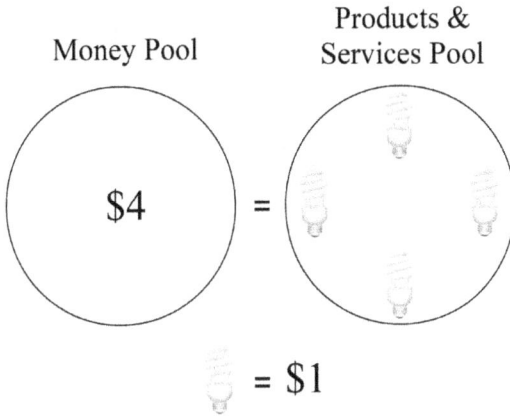

Money Pool   Products & Services Pool

$4 =

= $1

What if the government of this economy decided to inject more money into the economy and added another $1? What is the impact of this? What is the new value of each light bulb?

Well, each light bulb would now be worth $1.25.

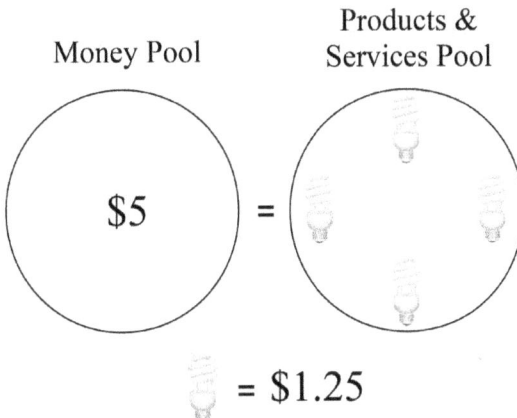

Money Pool   Products & Services Pool

$5 =

= $1.25

This is what inflation is. People and governments don't like inflation. It is not good for economies. The public will think that everything has become expensive and will stop buying.

Let's go back to our original example with 4 light bulbs and a money pool of $4.

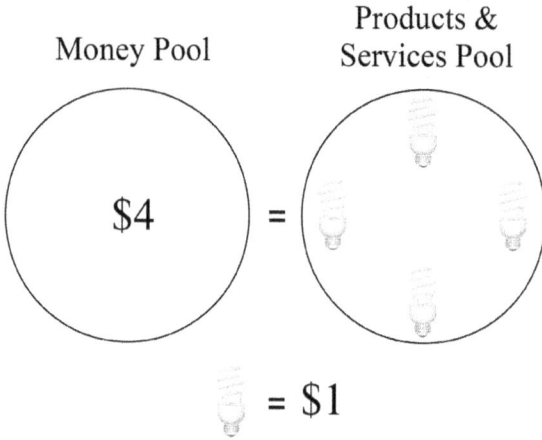

Money Pool

Products & Services Pool

$4 =

= $1

Now, what if an astute member of our economy was able to utilise their expertise and create another light bulb? What is the impact on our economy? How much is each light bulb worth?

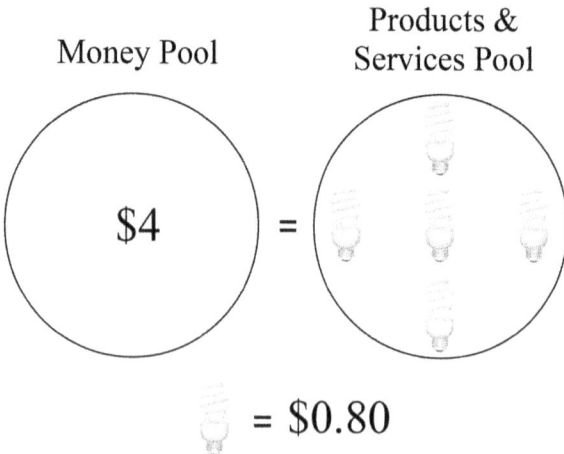

Money Pool

Products & Services Pool

$4 =

= $0.80

This is deflation. Governments and people do not like deflation. As with inflation, deflation is also bad for economies.

In the last example, to bring stability, the government would need to step in and add another $1 to the money pool.

The pools would then look like this:

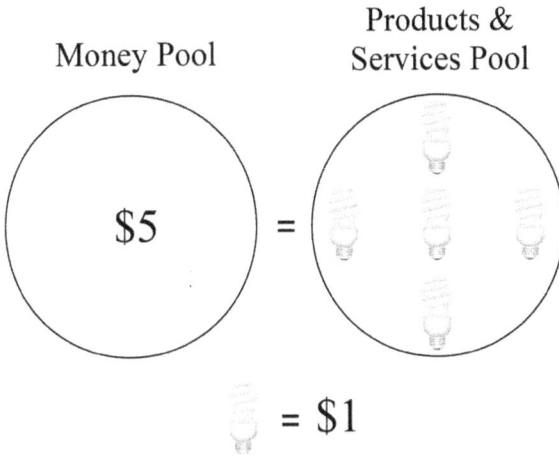

The economy is now back in balance.

At a basic level, this is how economies work. Governments manage the economy to keep inflation at a level that matches the amount of value that is being created.

There is just a much larger pool of money and a much larger pool of products and services.

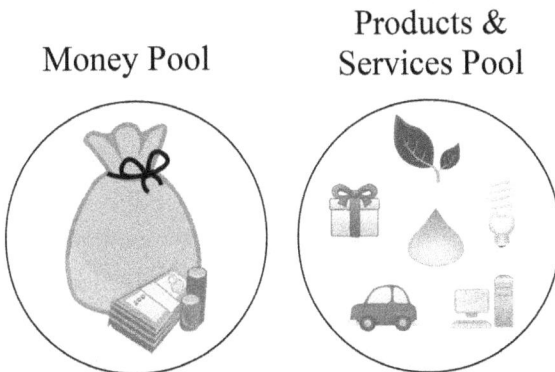

On a larger scale, all the money in all the countries in the world is the money pool, and all the goods and services in the world are the goods and services pool.

That is how the world economy works.

The thing to get clear on is that money still has no inherent value. Even on a global scale.

Wasting Money

It is interesting to note that spending money is good for society. It is just another name for trading. We often think that spending money is bad. That somehow something got wasted. It didn't. Spending money does not waste money. It is actually impossible to waste money. The money just goes to someone else. No matter for what you trade it. Whether you spend it on sex, drugs, rock and roll or a new Ferrari. The amount of assets in the world is the same. You just personally have less of them.

People often ask: "How can people spend money on a Ferrari when people in Africa are dying?". Comparing the two, however, does not make sense. The two things are completely unrelated. If everyone stopped buying Ferraris and gave the money to Africa, it doesn't necessarily mean that they will have more food. It just means that Ferrari will go into liquidation and less value will be created (as the Ferrari stakeholders will have a reduced capacity to create and capture value).

The problem of more food for Africa needs to be dealt with separately to the purchase of the Ferrari. Resolving this problem may have little to do with money.

No matter what you are trading, the main thing to ensure is that you are getting value for the money you are trading. Is the trade increasing your capacity to experience life, or reducing your capacity to experience life? Could you be creating more value by trading the money elsewhere? Either more value for yourself or for others. This may mean buying a Ferrari or giving it to an agency in Africa. That choice is for you.

How to Acquire More Money

There is a good reason why I am telling you all this.

If you want to have more money, you have two options:

1. You can try to get more money; or
2. You can create more value.

Number one you have probably already been trying. The question is: how do you get more money? Do you steal it or manipulate it from people? I wouldn't recommend it. Neither of these is going to work for very long.

Number two is the smarter option. It makes much more sense to create value.

Let's go back to our light bulb scenario.

There are still four light bulbs, and the total economy is worth \$4. Each light bulb is worth \$1, as before.

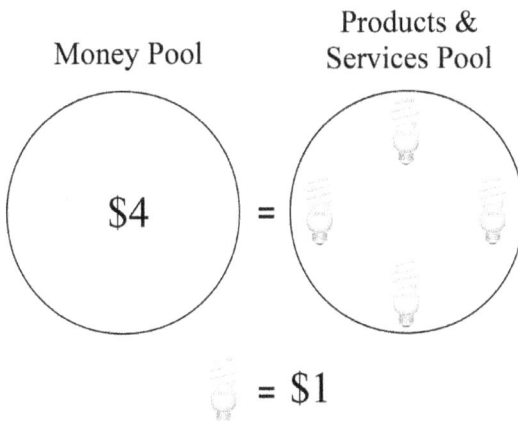

However in this scenario, John, Lucy, Sue and Eric each own one light bulb.

Money Pool

Products &
Services Pool

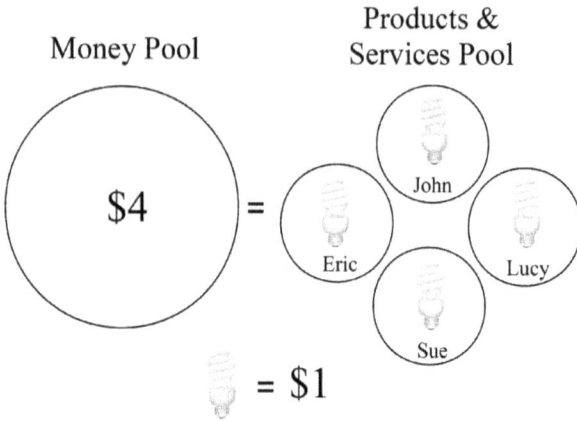

$4 =

= $1

Each person's share of this economy is $1.

Now, let's say Lucy is the enterprising person who created another light bulb. If the pool of money stays the same, each light bulb is now worth $0.80.

Money Pool

Products &
Services Pool

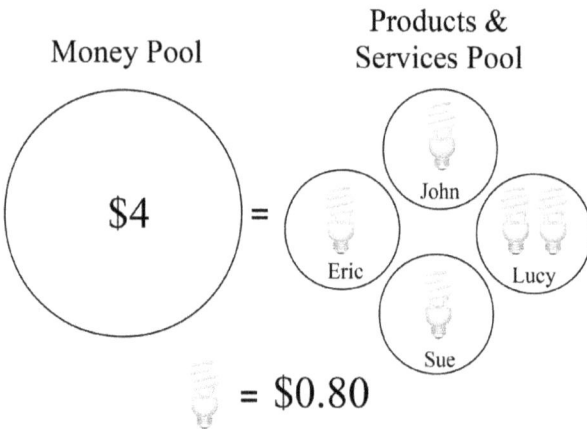

$4 =

= $0.80

Lucy is now worth $1.60. She has increased her share of the pool. She did not gain wealth by manipulating the market or by clever negotiation. She did it by creating value.

John, Eric and Sue then start complaining to the government about the deflation which has caused a decrease in the "value" of their assets, so the government steps in. It prints $1 and adds it to the economy.

The total value of the economy is now $5, and each light bulb is again valued at $1.

Money Pool

Products &
Services Pool

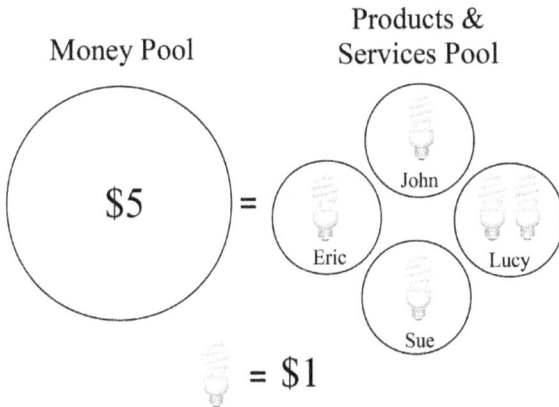

$5 =

John

Eric

Lucy

Sue

= $1

Everyone is now happy.

The major difference is for Lucy. She is the one who created the value (as a light bulb), and Lucy is now wealthier than she was before. She is now worth $2. She can use the assets for their own purpose, or trade them for dollars.

Although simplified, this is how economies work.

If you want more money, be like Lucy. Like Lucy, the access to increasing your share of the money pool is to create value. You add to the economy, you end up wealthier yourself and no one else loses out. This is a fundamental principle that is lost on most people. I repeat, Lucy became wealthier – *and no one else lost out.*

This is the difference between creating value and extracting value.

Creating value faster than the average of the rest of the world is what will give you an increase in money. If you have been increasing your wealth, you have almost certainly already been creating value. Whether you have been working for an employer, have your own business, or even if you are an investor. If you have been increasing your money, you have been creating value faster than the average person.

If your money has been reducing, it is because you have not been creating as much value as the average person.

I want to stress that creating value does not mean hard work. It may include hard work, but they are not necessarily related. There are people who work hard and create a lot of value, but there are people who work very hard and create little value. There are also people who create a great deal of value who don't work hard at all.

People often use the phrase: Don't work hard, work smart. I don't like that phrase. It never really gave me access to anything new. I prefer the phrase: Work hard or don't work hard; just make sure you are creating value.

The Magic Of Money – It's Power In A Marketplace

There is one particular quality to money that is more powerful than anything else. When I first got this, it blew my mind and had me fall in love with money.

To illustrate this, let's create a marketplace.

Let's say our farmer, Ben, goes to market with 100 pats of butter, which have an arbitrary usefulness to him of 50.

Ben's aim is to trade it for goods that have a higher usefulness to him than 50. That way he has increased his wealth. He goes to market and the following products are available: spinach, meat, fish and eggs.

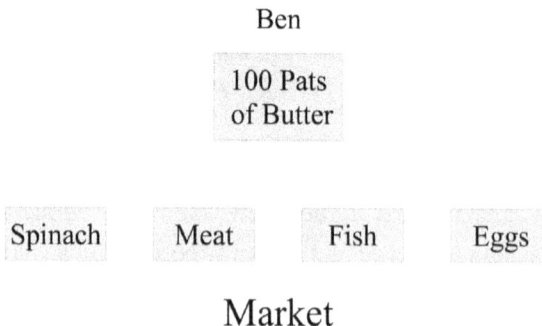

Ben

100 Pats
of Butter

Spinach   Meat   Fish   Eggs

Market

This market is based on a barter system.

What Ben really wants is meat. However, when Ben goes to the meat stall, the meat seller doesn't want to trade for any of Ben's butter. They don't like butter.

Ben now has a problem. This problem is known as the "double coincidence of wants". It basically says that a barter system requires two people to simultaneously want the item that the other person has. In a barter system, if you want meat, you don't just have to find someone who can supply you meat. You have to find someone who wants to supply you with meat and who also wants butter. Not a great basis for an efficient economy. This would seriously impact trade. Ben could only trade with stallholders who want butter.

Let's go back to the market and give each of the items a usefulness measure (utility) on behalf of Ben.

Ben

100 Pats
of Butter

Utility to Ben of 50

Market

Spinach	Meat	Fish	Eggs
Utility to Ben of 130	Utility to Ben of 400	Utility to Ben of 220	Utility to Ben of 180

At this market, the item with the biggest usefulness to Ben is the meat (with a utility of 400).

Lucy (the meat seller) doesn't want any butter. The only two people who want butter are Eric and John. John can trade his butter with Eric and receive eggs (which have a usefulness to him of 180) or trade with John and receive spinach (which has a usefulness to him of 130). It, obviously, makes sense for Ben to trade with Eric and receive the eggs (which have the higher usefulness of 180).

If we look at the situation from the point of view of utility, before going to market, Ben's butter had a utility for him of 50. Once at market, however, Ben's butter had a utility for him of 180 (because it could be traded for items that had a utility of 180). This brings us to a valuable statement.

In a marketplace, the utility of an item is the equivalent of the highest utility of any item for which it can be traded.

Now let's bring in a standard currency (money).

By introducing a standard currency, we deal with the problem of the "double coincidence of wants" beautifully. Any trader can now trade with any other trader. Ben can sell his items (for money) to anyone who wants butter. Ben can then use that money to buy meat. This makes trading much more efficient.

Let's look at the example of Ben going to market again.

Ben

100 Pats
of Butter

Market Price $80
(Utility to Ben of 50)

Market

Spinach	Meat	Fish	Eggs
Market Price $80 (Utility to Ben of 130)	Market Price $80 (Utility to Ben of 400)	Market Price $80 (Utility to Ben of 220)	Market Price $80 (Utility to Ben of 180)

Ben sells his butter for $80. He then goes to Lucy and buys meat with the $80 which has a utility of 400. By selling his butter for money rather than bartering it, Ben was greatly able to increase the utility of his butter in this marketplace.

As we said earlier, in a marketplace, the utility of an item is the equivalent of the highest utility of any item for which it can be traded. Given that money is so widely accepted, the utility of money in a marketplace is incredibly high.

Because money is so universally accepted, it makes it much easier for us to trade. The easier it is to trade, the more value can be created. This is the real value of money. Once money became available to society, it greatly increased the speed and ease with which we could create wealth.

It is still the creation of value that is the important piece, though.

Money doesn't make the world go around. Value makes the world go around. Money just makes it happen faster.

PART 4

Leverage

Ownership

Understanding the conversations I have created in this book is one thing. The intention, however, is for you to be able to take these conversations and become someone who creates a great deal of value in your life.

One of the biggest blocks that gets in the way of people fulfilling their potential is their inability to own their own value. Until you experience your own value and are strongly connected to your own value, it is almost impossible for you to capitalise on it.

Your Value

One of the things I have found in my journey is that I will only become as wealthy as I believe I deserve to be. If I don't believe I deserve wealth in an area of life, it is difficult for me to let it in.

It is, therefore, very important that I get in touch with my own personal value to the world.

We all have an inherent value, and most of us need to do a lot of work to get in touch with this.

Your experience of your own value will have started in childhood, when you first became conscious of yourself as a separate being. You would have made decisions about what you were good at, or not good at. Decisions about your value to your family and to the world.

I personally think that each generation has its own flavour of this.

In my grandfather's day, the value of an individual life was not given the respect it is given today. In the First and Second World Wars, people were sacrificed in their millions. It was seen then as a fair price to pay.

By the sixties, this kind of trade no longer made sense to many people. During the Vietnam War, people started to protest. Soldiers would tell stories of the emotional impact of the actions they had taken in battle. The perceived value of a life had increased, and the trade no longer made sense to many people.

When people were protesting, however, I believe they were protesting for an acknowledgement of the value of all life. Their own included.

In western culture, it now requires more and more justification to take lives.

My generation has its own flavour. When I grew up, it was partly expected that children were seen and not heard. Society did not regard children as fully developed people. They needed to be trained first. There was a belief that children are generally unruly and, without structure and rules, they would not fit into society. It was customary for children to be smacked by parents. If we broke the rules at school, we would be forced to stand at the front of the class, hold out both hands and be struck with a long, wide leather strap (corporal punishment). I remember when they outlawed corporal punishment in the United Kingdom. Many parents were up in arms. Everyone expected that there would be chaos in schools. I remember hearing someone say, "How will they be able to control the kids without belting them?"

All of this is a reflection of the relationship between adults and kids back then. It was the background relationship of western society. It seems inappropriate now, however, that way of thinking was appropriate to the time. One of the impacts of this way of relating to children is that, from the child's point of view, they don't experience being inherently valuable. I know in growing up, I experienced society's pressure to get results in school and be a particular way in life. It seemed that my main value to society was in what I produced. Fortunately, I was either very stubborn, or I had other strong connections that helped me to not lose touch completely with my own value. It was most likely a little of both.

Since then, society's relationship to children has changed. I believe we are more open to the value of diversity, and find it less necessary to mould our children. It is probably one of the biggest shifts within my generation. Although this has left many parents scrambling with no idea of how we can at least maintain the "pretence" that we know what we are doing (certainly this is my experience), I think the shift is an incredibly valuable one.

As with adults, the more aware a child becomes of their own value, the greater their capacity to create value. Encouraging this awareness in a new generation of children holds great possibility for the future of society.

What Is Your Value?

When I took time off to spend with my children, I found aspects of it very confronting. One of the things I noticed was how hard I found it to do "nothing". Now obviously, I wasn't doing nothing – I was taking care of my children. However, for someone who had spent most of his life being driven by results, it seemed like I was doing nothing. A big part of me wanted, more needed, to feel like I was doing things that would lead to a specific result. I realised that I was addicted to "doing". My whole identity was based around how good I was at producing results. Although I had a strong desire to spend time with my children, I craved to be "doing something".

No matter what, I *felt* more valuable when I was doing something. Even if what I was doing created no value, it somehow seemed more appropriate to be doing.

During this period at home, I asked myself, "Who am I if I produce no results? If I produce no results, do I still have value?".

I explored this for a long period before I developed a new relationship to myself.

Here is what I realised: I am not my results. My value to society is not in my results. I have an inherent value.

Exercise

I want you to do an exercise.

First, close your eyes. Take a few minutes to get comfortable and relaxed.

Now, I want you to think of someone really important to you in your life. Imagine you are with them; you are doing something you like to do with them. Feel the experience of being with them.

Take a few minutes to get present to the experience of being around that person.

Now imagine they have an appointment to go to. They leave. Fifteen minutes later, you receive a phone call that they have been hit by a car and have been killed. You will never, ever see them again.

This may be confronting, but take a few minutes to experience the impact.

I have a question for you: what is the loss that you now feel?

What will you miss most about that person? What will you never experience again? What will no longer be available to you now that the person is gone?

It is unlikely that what you miss will be the results that person produced or the clothes they wore. What you will miss most about that person goes much deeper.

If they were a good singer, having a CD of them singing would not satisfy your desire to be with them.

It is the feeling of being with them that you will miss. The experience of their energy. How you feel when you are around them. The feeling when they walk into a room. Their ability to connect with you and your connection with them. The feeling of loss when they walk away.

Everyone has an essence and an energy which is wholly their own.

Now, there is a second part of the exercise. I want you to imagine that you are with the same person. This time, however, you are the one who has to go to the appointment. You are the one who is hit by a car and killed. The other person is the one who gets the call.

This person will feel exactly the same way you did. What they miss about you will not be how much you earned, how neat your hair was or how thin you were. It will be deeper than that. They will miss your energy. Your essence. How they felt when you were around.

That is your true value to the world. This is the way to measure your value.

To know the value of something, you need to experience what it is like when it is no longer around. You need to have contrast.

That is why many people struggle to experience their own value.

The reality is that you are never going to fully experience your own value. It is impossible. I experience your value because I have contrast. I know how it felt before you walked into the room, and I know how it feels when you walk out again. I know what it feels like when you are around, and I know what it feels like when you are not.

You will never, ever experience your own value. You will never know what it feels like when you are not around. For you, you are always there. You may get a sense that you have value, but you will never fully experience it.

It doesn't mean that the value isn't there, though.

If you go by your experience of your own value, you will have a very small life. There is little connection between your experience of your own value and your actual value to the world.

This is incredibly powerful to get. When you can let go of your own experience of your value, you are able to become interested in what the people in your world experience as your value.

Your energy and your presence are more valuable than all the things for which you think you are valued.

Check out this link to get a sense of the inherent value of one person. One of the many video responses to Juan Mann's original Free Hugs Campaign. As you watch the video, you may be impacted by how valuable connecting with another is.

https://youtu.be/DugeQ6vkC6Y

Time

When you have worked with the distinctions of value, another thing you will become aware of is that the greatest resource you have is your time.

It is the one thing that is truly limited for you in your life. You are already dying. You have less life left now than you did 10 seconds ago. This may seem like bad news, but the good news is that you probably still have lots of time left.

What will make the difference is what you do with it.

As you become more aware of value and the trades you are making in your life, you will also become more discerning about what you do with your time.

Your time is your most valuable resource. What you choose to spend this resource on is going to make the biggest difference to your wealth, and the wealth of those around you. It makes more sense to trade with people with whom you are going to create the most value. Thinking in these terms is not selfish. Remember, both parties benefit from a trade that creates value. If you are not creating value with someone, you are wasting both your and their time. Find the people you can create value with.

It is interesting that when people are employed, they think they are selling their time when they are not. As we have previously said, they may be giving their time, but that is not for what their employer is paying them.

Your time is of no use to anyone. Stop thinking you are selling your time. If you think you are selling time, you are never going to be wealthy. Partly because your time is limited but, more importantly, because you are disconnected from the value you are creating for your employer.

This leads to a lot of inefficiency. People spend a day in an office when they could actually create the result in two hours. In the traditional way of looking at employment, the person might then spend the rest of the day killing time on the internet or staring out of the window. This is one of the most demoralising scenarios for a human being. There is no benefit to you or your client/employer in this. Instead, find a way to sell the result to your employer (or client if you are self-employed). It will be better for both you and them. When you sell your client time, it costs them time. Time in a chair, time with them — you end up being a pain in the neck. Find a way to get your client the result they want, with as little fuss as possible, and they will receive more value from you. If you are in a role like this, I recommend you read the *The 4-Hour Workweek* by Timothy Ferriss. It has many great examples of how you can leverage the value you create in less time.

Health

If time is your most valuable resource, the biggest thing you can do to increase the amount of time you have available is to take care of your health. Your health is the second most valuable commodity you have – it gives you more time.

What you do with your body, what you put in your body and how you get the best out of your body are going to drastically impact the amount of time you have on the planet and the quality of your time on the planet.

Taking good care of your health is important not just for you, but for the others around you.

Society needs you to be healthy. You create value.

The people around you need you.

Performance As A Self-Expression

One of the distinctions I created in one of my previous programs was called Performance as a Self-Expression. Your self-expression is one of your greatest resources. If you are doing exactly what you want to be doing in any moment, that is when you will have the greatest output. It takes little energy to do exactly what you feel like doing. It happens naturally.

Most of us were not trained to work that way. We were trained to suppress what we really want to do and force ourselves to do something we really don't want to do.

What is strange is that, in a persons working day, most of the energy is not expended on the activity that the person is doing. Most of the energy is expended on suppressing what the person really wants to be doing so that they can do what they don't want to do.

Holding back your self-expression takes a lot of energy.

It makes much more sense to release your self-expression.

To have your self-expression be the force that drives your life.

You Don't Need To Give Anything Up

Using your self-expression as a driving force in your life is not as big a switch as it sounds. Performance as a self-expression doesn't mean that you have to leave your job, your marriage or your friends.

If you are the CEO of a large organisation who is married with a family and a mortgage, it doesn't necessarily mean you should leave it all and become a musician.

It is about looking at who you are naturally. Your natural self-expression. Then it is a case of creating avenues where this self-expression will forward your aims

The great thing is that, along the way, you develop a deeper connection to yourself.

The more connected you are to "who you are", the more freedom you will have to express it in your professional role — and in any area of life. It is rarely the role that is the constraint. If your self-expression is to connect with people, you can do this as a musician or as a CEO. Each role would benefit from an increased ability to connect with others.

Once you get in touch with what your natural expression is, you will likely find that your self-expression creates more value in some areas than others, and with some people more than others.

Don't worry about that yet. That will take care of itself later as you expand your awareness of–and ability to create–value. For the moment, learning to release, and work from, your self-expression will add more value than worrying about where it will be expressed.

Relationships

Relationships Are Key To Wealth

Let's think back to our examples earlier with Bill and Ben.

What is clear is that both benefit from the trades they make each week.

One of the things which is important, however, is that prior to Bill and Ben trading, they needed to establish a relationship. Without Bill and Ben establishing a relationship, there is no possibility of trading. It is possible for them to never have communicated with each other and there would be no capacity to trade. In order for them to trade and create value with each other, they first need to create some form of relationship. Whether they bump into each other outside their farms one day, are introduced through others, find each other on the internet, or some other way is irrelevant. What is important is that they establish a relationship.

Relationships are the foundation of wealth creation. No matter what form of currency the wealth is in: love, tennis, music, sex, business or money.

When you get in touch with the value that you provide for others, and that others provide for you, you will get a whole new access to wealth.

This was something I realised when I first started consulting. I can have the best ideas that have the potential to dramatically impact the business community, have a great positive impact on people and transform the planet. The ideas themselves, however, make no difference. The creation of value through using the ideas only happens when they impact other people. It happens in partnership with others. I could have the best products in the world, but if no one knows who I am and what I have got to offer, then I will have no impact.

The Relationship Is More Valuable Than What You Are Trading

Think about this. Value is created by trading with a client. However, on a deeper level, the value is in the relationship you have with your client. The relationship creates a channel. Once you have created a channel that you can trade through, you have infinite opportunities to create value – either now or in the future. Once you know the client and what will create the most value in the relationship, you can capitalise on the relationship which will benefit both of you.

The More Relationships You Have, The More Value You Can Create

One of the things that becomes apparent is that the number of relationships you have directly affects your capacity to create value.

If you have a million litres of water, but only a relationship with one thirsty person, you can create limited value.

If you have a million litres of water and relationships with a million thirsty people, you can create a great deal more value.

The People Around You Matter

It has often been said that if you want to know your net worth, find the net worth of the five people with whom you spend the most time. Add their net worth, divide it by 5, and it will give you your net worth.

It makes a lot of sense.

You can only create value by trading something that is available in your community.

If there is a lack of food in your community, it is going to be difficult for you to acquire food. In the same way, if there is a lack of money in your community, it is going to be difficult for you to acquire money. That is why many people want to be selling ideas to corporate markets. In a corporate market, money is a readily available resource.

If you want to increase your wealth in a particular currency, the easiest way to do it is to find a community that has an abundance of that resource.

I Make You Rich – You Make Me Rich

This type of relationship awareness leads to the possibility of awesome relationships. Relationships can now exist for you on an "I make you rich – you make me rich" basis, whether it be a business or a personal relationship. When you understand relationships this way, and develop a desire to make those around you rich, other people will be a lot more likely to trade with you. It doesn't matter what the currency is.

This is now the basis on which I do business with people. Before entering a business arrangement, I first want to know if the other party is genuinely interested in increasing my wealth. I know that my wealth increases through creating value for the other, and I want to know if they think the same way.

Trading What You Have Most Of For What You Have Least Of

It makes sense that in relationships often opposites attract. It is no accident.

If you are smart but a bit boring, it makes more sense to be in a relationship with someone who is silly and fun. Although you will probably clash with each other, you intuitively experience the value of the relationship. The biggest way to increase wealth is to trade what you have most of for what you have least of.

It also makes sense why people who are old and have a lot of money get together with people who are young and have little money. Each person is providing a currency they have an abundance of and receiving a resource they have little of.

In many ways, personal relationships are not that different from business relationships.

Both are marketplaces that create value.

Marketplaces

Why The Farmer Went To Market

If you understand the benefit of relationships to increasing your capacity to create wealth, you will be able to work out the real benefit of a marketplace.

Let's define what I mean by a marketplace. A marketplace is any place where two people trade.

It could be Bill and Ben getting together once a week.

It could be the whole community getting together at a farmers market.

It could be a bar where people go to meet each other.

A romantic relationship is a marketplace.

Marketplaces exist because they create value. A marketplace is a value-creating entity.

A farmer brings his "value as butter" which has little use to him, and trades it for "value as money" (sells it). He then trades the "value as money" for "value as meat" (or fish, bread, etc.).

On the other side of this transaction, another farmer brings his "value as meat", trades it for "value as money" (sells it), then trades the "value as money" for "value as fish" (or butter, bread, etc).

Everyone in a marketplace benefits. Everyone experiences an increase in wealth. The usefulness of what they receive is greater than the usefulness of what they gave. If it wasn't, there would be no point in going to market.

Not only that, the value that is created in a marketplace is so great that there is enough to pay a share of the created value to the owner of the marketplace.

Example

Bill brings butter, which has a usefulness to him of 100. He sells 90% of his butter for $50. He pays the market owner the other 10% of the butter as commission. He then buys $50 worth of meat which to him has a usefulness of 200.

Ben brings meat, which has a usefulness to him of 100. He sells 90% of his meat for $50. He pays the market owner the other 10% of the meat as commission. He then buys $50 worth of bread which to him has a usefulness of 200.

Other examples are bars. People go to bars to meet people. They go out and spend money on drinks or food. However the currency they are interested in is connection, friendship, love or sex.

The bar or restaurant owner owns the marketplace. They are the ones who profit from the value that gets created from bringing the customers together.

The Power Of The Market Owner

If you look at the previous example or, in fact, any example, of a marketplace, the person who has the most power is the person who controls the marketplace. This person is the one who has control over whether the other parties get to create value or not.

As an extreme example, the market owner can charge 90% of the created value and allow the other parties 5% of the created value each, and it would still be beneficial for the trading parties to come to market.

This is very important to get.

This is the part that allows someone to profit massively from transactions. It is this that allows certain players to profit financially over and above the other parties.

If you are the one creating the market, you are the one with the power.

Of course, in reality, it is not quite so simple. Supply and demand also have an impact on marketplaces.

Buyers' Market

This is the same when people talk about a buyers' market. In a buyers' market, buyers have the power. Usually it is because there are more sellers of a product than there are buyers for the product.

The key thing to understand, however, is that the buyers end up controlling the marketplace. They can choose with whom to create value.

Sellers' Market

In a sellers' market, sellers have the power. Usually it is because there are more buyers of a product than there are sellers of a product.

The key thing to understand, however, is that the sellers end up controlling the marketplace. They can choose with whom to create value.

The Value In Creating A Market For You

Given that the person who controls the marketplace is the one with the power and, therefore, the person who is most likely to profit, it makes sense to be the one who is holding the commodity that people want. This is one of the reasons why famous people are able to get wealthy. They control the marketplace for their own brand.

This is also one of the reasons there has been such an upsurge in people who are using online media to develop a personal brand:

When you are the one that creates the value, there is no competitor.

When you are the one people want, there is no substitute.

When you are the one people want, there is no way for anyone else to control the market.

When you control the marketplace, you are able to dictate how much value you capture.

If you can connect with your natural self-expression, find where it creates value in the world, and capture a portion of the created value, then you can have the makings of a good business.

It's just different from the traditional way we think of business.

PART 5

Business

Business as a Marketplace

A Value-Creating Entity

As we discussed in the last chapter, a marketplace is a value-creating entity. The only reason it exists is because it creates value. It is easier for a hundred people to meet in a specific place at a specific time than to arrange for them to all meet individually. A marketplace provides more value than the alternative of individuals meeting up separately to trade.

Business As A Marketplace

This is what a business is. All businesses are marketplaces. No matter if it is a lemonade stall that has been set up by one of my kids, or one of the largest multi-national organisations (Apple, Facebook, Microsoft and banks such as JP Morgan), the principles are the same.

In a child's lemonade stall, they bring together the following resources:

- A table
- Paper and coloured pens (for a sign)
- Lemons
- Water

- Sugar
- Ice
- Cups
- Manpower
- Sales expertise
- Weather information

In the lemonade stall, it costs 50¢ to produce one cup (of lemonade), and it is priced to sell at $2. The customer comes along and purchases the lemonade because they receive more value in the lemonade (or from the smile on the child's face when they purchase the lemonade) than the $2 they pay.

The child has made $1.50 per cup, less a portion for any fixed costs.

The bringing together of the resources and the customer create a marketplace. The child is the one who creates the marketplace and takes $1.50 per cup sold for the creation of it.

A multi-national organisation is the same thing. The marketplace is just bigger and connects more resources.

It brings together:

- Investors with an investment (shareholders)
- Experts with a place to be rewarded for their expertise (staff)
- Customers and products (sales)
- Suppliers and needs (procurement)
- Etc.

Bringing together these resources creates value, and each person who is involved in the marketplace captures a portion of that value.

A business is a beautiful, almost spiritual entity. Its existence creates value. People often don't realise it because they are so focussed on looking at a business from a financial viewpoint that they fail to see what a business actually is.

It is a value-creating entity.

Business Is Not About Making Money

Business is not about making money. It really isn't. It just looks that way.

Business is no more about making money than basketball is about shooting hoops.

What Is The Real Purpose Of A Game Of Basketball?

Is the purpose of a game of basketball to shoot as many hoops as possible?

No, it isn't. Basketball is not about shooting hoops.

It just looks that way.

There is no value in putting a ball through a metal ring. It makes no difference to humanity, and there is nothing to get excited about. I could walk over to a local empty basketball court, shoot the ball through a hoop, and there would be no impact on myself or humanity. Nobody would cheer or get excited. It isn't even that hard to do.

Yet there is a multi-billion dollar industry built around the game of basketball. Therefore, there must be billions of dollars of value getting created.

Where is the value created?

As in most sports, the objective is irrelevant. Whether it is kicking an oblong ball between two metal posts (Australian rules football) or running it over a particular line at one stage of a game (rugby or gridiron), the rules of the game themselves are made up and often inherently irrelevant. They can even change from season to season.

The rules can change because the objective itself has no value. What has value is that there *is* an objective, and that there are other people to compete with to achieve the objective.

It is the competing that provides access to creating value.

Where is the value created?

The value for the teams is in their experience of life while trying to achieve their objective. To get *better* at achieving their objective. To test themselves to see how good they can get. To test themselves physically, mentally, energetically, emotionally and maybe even spiritually.

The value for the spectators is in the excitement of watching the game. The sense of belonging to a tribe of fans. Of having somewhere to go on a Friday night. Of having something to talk about with their buddies.

For the television networks, the value is in the number or people watching and the pay subscriptions, or the revenue from advertisers.

The purpose of the game is not to shoot a ball through a hoop. The purpose of the game is to create value. Playing a competitive game creates more value than a nation sitting down at home doing nothing.

For the players, becoming good at the game takes more than just an ability to stand and shoot a ball through a basket. To compete in the game of basketball takes fitness, agility, strength of character, competitiveness, focus and an ability to handle pressure.

Shooting the ball through a hoop is not the purpose of basketball. It is just a measure that allows us to gauge the effectiveness of all these other elements of the game.

The Game Of Business

Business is the same. Business is not about making money. No more than basketball is about shooting hoops.

Making a profit is not the game. It is a measure of your effectiveness in the game.

The profit you make is a reflection of the value you are creating.

Being effective in the game of business is all about your ability to create value. Whether that be for your employees, your shareholders, your customers or the public at large.

To do that takes becoming highly effective at communication, personnel management, financial management, marketing, etc. All of these are elements that create value.

Perceived Value Vs. Real Value

There are, of course, a number of people and businesses that exaggerate the value of the products or services they produce. This is another impact of living in a world that has a primary background context of "money is important".

There are businesses out there that are literally poisoning their customers. CEOs and business owners who think that their role is to sell as much of their product as possible, even if the product is detrimental to people's health.

There is just no need for it. Many companies misunderstand the value they provide for their customers. In some fast food chains, for instance, the products do not create value in one of the most fundamental currencies in which food is meant to create value: the currency of health.

Many fast food chains are extracting value rather than creating value. By not genuinely creating value, their customers are worse off after doing business with them.

Often, it is thought that there is little that can be done because the value is in the product, which just happens to be unhealthy. In reality, however, customers are rarely only attracted by a product. In fast food chains, for instance, there are many currencies being exchanged when buying a product. People may buy the item because of the experience in the restaurant, the connection with the marketing, the speed of delivery or the price. Having unhealthy food is not often a *necessary* requirement.

There are many fast food chains that are currently dealing with the impact of this way of doing business. Some were created in a different era, when consumers were not so value conscious. As consumers have become more conscious of value, there are chains struggling to stay in business.

Business people cannot avoid the fact that business is fundamentally about creating value. If you are not creating value, you should not be in business.

Perceived value does not create value. It just looks like it creates value. If your relationships with your customers are not creating real value, your relationships are going to be short term and the more you trade with your clients, the less wealthy they will be. This is one of the impacts of living in a society that has a money-based view of the world. If you have a money-based view, you will experience the world as limited. It will then seem that, for you to get what you want, there has to be a cost to another, and the cost to others will be justified.

This is a screwed up context, though.

Why would you do that when you could be creating real value? Real value creates wealth. For both parties. The more you trade with your clients, the wealthier they will be, and the wealthier you will be. These are relationships that will last long term. Value is unlimited. Both parties in the trade win. There is no need for anyone else to be worse off. When you understand this, it makes no sense to do business any other way.

Value Extraction

There are other impacts which come from the win/lose view of business.

Rather than creating a business as a tool to create value, people who see business as a win/lose game often create a business to extract value. Value extraction is when you are taking more value than you are creating.

Many people think that this is what business is about. This is something of which it is important for you to be aware. Especially if you are an investor who finds themselves listening to people pitching business ideas.

In reality, value extraction is not that difficult to spot. People who operate in this realm will generally only be talking in terms of money. They will be talking about how much money you can make. Of course, you now know that it is not possible to make money. Anyone who is talking in terms of making money (which is a lot of people) does not understand how money works and will likely be "making money" off of you through extraction. Once you become someone who is aware of value, you'll be able to understand whether someone is creating value or extracting value. You will be able to see if value is getting created in both sides of the transaction. In any successful business model, value has to be created.

Get Rich Quick Schemes

Over the years, I have come across many different "wealth creation" schemes. Many of these are run by people who offer programs that purport to make you money. Once you understand how wealth is really created, programs like this lose their appeal. It becomes much easier to recognise that there is no value being created; only value being extracted. It is also likely that value is being extracted from you.

If the other party is not creating value, you want to be extremely wary. Ask them where the value is getting created. If they look at you strangely, you know to walk away. You've got to see where the value is getting created.

I'm not saying it's impossible in the short term to end up with more money, but why would you play that way? On-going, it will be difficult, if not impossible, for you to keep money until you understand how to create value.

If somebody comes to me with a business transaction, the first thing I want to know is "where does value get created?" People can think that their idea is brilliant, and it may be brilliant. However, all

I am interested in is, "where does the value get created?". If value isn't getting created somewhere in that transaction, then there will be no value to be captured and it will not be a viable business.

If you're unsure whether value can be created, write down the transaction as a whole. Write down each side of the transaction. Write down where value is getting created. Write down where the value can be captured.

Value extraction doesn't create anything for the world and people can feel it. Intuitively, people know the difference between value creation and value extraction. You'll pick up the sense of why somebody is doing what they do. Trust yourself. You don't need to extract money to become rich.

When I grew up in the UK in the 70s and 80s, there were some large characters on television. Two, in particular, became a large part of UK culture, Arthur Daley (from *Minder*) and Del Boy (from *Only Fools & Horses*). These characters were highly lovable and were always trying to make money. They would get involved in hilarious get rich quick schemes that would always backfire. The shows were very funny, but there was also an element of sadness for me in watching. There was a sense of desperation and frustration.

In both cases, the Arthur Daley character and the Del Boy character were people who were committed to making a difference. They were people who wanted to make an impact in the world, and they were frustrated and thwarted in that. Even though they are fictional television characters, they represent a lot of people in the world who are committed to making a big difference and committed to having an impact, and are ultimately thwarted. Thwarted by the conversation of money and the inability to be powerful with it.

People intuitively feel that something is "not quite right" when people have their attention on "making money". They may think that money is wrong. But it's not money that's wrong. It is the context we have for money. Money is incredibly powerful, but people give it respect in areas that it doesn't deserve, and don't give it respect in areas that it does deserve.

This is what thwarts people. Trying all sorts of things to make money, rather than using their skills to create value. If they had the distinctions of creating value, it would be a whole different ballgame.

A similar real life character is Jordan Belfort. If you read the book *The Wolf of Wall Street*, or watched the movie, Jordan Belfort was obviously someone who had a potential to create value. He was a highly effective salesperson, and great at motivating and inspiring people and his staff.

The problem was that his context was wrong. He was in the world of value extraction rather than value creation. It had a massive impact on both himself and others. He spent 22 months in a federal prison. If you see pictures of him, he doesn't look like someone who's inspired by himself or what he created.

Given a different background context for wealth, he could have used his skills to make an enormous difference to others. It is possible he still could.

People who are in the world of value extraction can't survive indefinitely in business. The people they are extracting value from are usually their customers. If every time I trade with you, you are worse off, I can only keep doing business with you for a limited period of time.

If every time I trade with you we are both better off, we can keep doing business forever.

Your Business Is Not Only For You

To build a successful business, you have to be able to see beyond yourself. There are so many factors that need to come together in a successful business, and many of the people you are interacting with do not have making you wealthy as their number one priority.

Everyone who interacts with a business on any level does so because it creates value for them.

Therefore, your business has a much greater impact on the community than you realise.

The College

In 2010, I sold the college I owned and spent the next few years at home with my family.

In 2013, however, I heard that the college had gone into receivership. This impacted me for a few reasons.

First, there was the impact of dealing with the fact that something I had previously put a lot of energy into was no longer in existence.

Second, I was owed a large amount of money from the college owners.

Third, and this was the main impact, a marketplace had disappeared.

While the college was trading, a marketplace existed where students would come and pay fees to receive education. Friendships would be formed. People would develop themselves personally and professionally. Social groups were created. Students would learn and develop skills that would allow them to go out into the world and create value for others over a period of years.

Also, the college lecturers and staff would come and provide expertise, receive satisfaction from teaching others, be trained and pushed by the students and receive "value as money" for their services.

There may have been a financial impact for those responsible for the college at the time it went into liquidation. However, there was a greater impact on the community. The community lost a marketplace. A marketplace that created value.

No Longer Creating Value

In reality, however, it is likely that the college failed because the business was no longer creating value.

This is why business owners need to be highly aware of value, and where value is being created by their business in the marketplace. Your ability to create value can change very quickly.

During the period I owned the college, the courses the business offered were at the premium end of the market. The college used to charge $9000 for a course that was offered for $5500 elsewhere. We were able to charge that amount because we created a great deal of value.

In 2009, it was announced that the next year the government would be paying around 80% of the fees. They did, however, cap the fees at $6000. The college was not allowed to charge more than this $6000. Within 12 months, our business model had to change drastically. Our ability to create value in the marketplace was seriously curtailed, as was our ability to capture value.

Being aware of value is essential to making good business decisions. Markets can change very quickly.

Building a Value-Based Business

Entrepreneurship

Becoming aware of value is essential for entrepreneurs.

It is at the heart of what an entrepreneur does. People may say they spotted a "gap" in the market, but what they are really saying is that they spotted an opportunity to create value in a marketplace. They can only spot "gaps" (opportunities to create value) when they are "value aware".

The ability to see opportunities to create value, then pull together the resources to create that value, then to structure deals to capture a portion of that value, is integral to the creation of new business.

I meet many people who would like to set up a business of their own. Usually they fall into two camps:

1. People who are aware of value.

   They have no "great idea". They don't even care about having a great idea. They may have no skills either. What they are good at, however, is creating value. These people rarely talk about the businesses they are creating. There is nothing to talk about. They see an opportunity to create value and they fill it.

2. People who are not aware of value.

Generally, these people have great ideas and plans, but no business. I understand how alluring this can be. Business people from the outside look like they have great ideas (and sometimes they do have great ideas). It is not the greatness of the idea that creates the successful business, though. It is whether the idea creates value.

If you want to set up a business of your own, make sure you are in group 1. Start with where you can create value.

Lean Thinking

The whole idea of lean start-up and lean thinking (check out the book *Lean Start-up* by Eric Ries) is based on value-based methodologies. The question that lean thinking tries to answer is, "How do we create as much value as possible with as little resources as possible?" Lean thinking has altered the way many people relate to business.

Before lean thinking, a traditional business strategy would be to come up with an idea, create a business plan, borrow money from the bank, set up a shop and start trading.

The problem with this approach is that when you start up in business, all you have is an idea. An idea itself will never create wealth; you need to find out whether implementing the idea creates value. If you can create value in the marketplace, that is when you have the makings of a business.

You can't know this, however, until your idea is out there in the marketplace. In the end, it is the marketplace that decides whether your idea has value or not.

Lean start-up methodologies recommend creating a minimum viable product as quickly as possible and then testing this product for value in the marketplace. The feedback you get from the marketplace then allows you to adjust quickly and retest the market as necessary.

Lean methodologies are very efficient because they allow you to follow where the value is. You are constantly testing for value.

You can bring a product to market quickly and cheaply without having to remortgage your house first. You can test the product in different markets and get feedback for your next iteration. Lean methodologies are all to support you in finding out where you can provide the most value.

I am constantly surprised by the number of people I meet whose first experience of business was borrowing hundreds of thousands of dollars from a family member, setting up a business without any testing of the idea, then falling in a heap six months later.

There is a place for bold moves in business, but there is no need to start a business this way. Particularly in current times, when ideas can be tested so easily.

Start-ups that follow lean methodologies are generally much more flexible, dynamic and less risky than start-ups that follow the traditional route. In principle, they are more closely related to what actually makes a business successful.

Increasing The Value Of Your Business

If you are interested in increasing the value of your business, creating more value is key.

Creating value increases your ability to capture value, which, in turn, increases your potential for profit, which then increases the value of your business.

The value of your business in dollar terms is linked to the value your business creates in the marketplace.

The more value you create for your customers, the more value you will be able to capture (as money).

The more value you create for your staff in the currencies that are important to them, the happier your staff will be and the more value you can capture as performance.

The more value you create in the community, the more you can shout about the value you are creating, and the more people will know to come to you to create that value.

Creating A Value-Based Culture

When a business operates within the distinctions of value, the culture of the business changes. The conversations change, the motivations change and the general feel of the business changes. The main difference between a business that operates inside the distinctions of value and one that does not is that, in a value aware business, the staff are clear on both the value the business creates and the value that they, as a staff member, create.

When a staff member knows they are making a difference in their role, for both the organisation and for the world – when they experience providing value – they have more at stake.

When the distinctions of value are alive in an organisation, staff are more inspired, innovative and cohesive. Your staff will experience the purpose of the organisation. You will also attract others who connect with your purpose.

Simon Sinek has a famous TED talk called *How Great Leaders Inspire Action* (more commonly known as *Start with Why*). You can watch the video here: https://youtu.be/sioZd3AxmnE.

It is a great TED talk which, in very simple terms, articulates the power of people being connected to a purpose.

One of the problems for many businesses is that the management themselves are disconnected from the purpose of their business. How can you expect your staff to be connected to the purpose of the organisation if you are not connected to it yourself?

Whether you are connected to it or not, your business does have a purpose. Given that it already has a purpose, wouldn't it make sense to have yourself and your staff deeply connected to this purpose?

Your business is not only for you.

Business Success

To be successful in business takes more than focussing on money, even if from the outside it looks like that is all business people are focussed on. Just because someone has a Lamborghini or a big house, does not mean that having the Lamborghini or the big house is what drives them. In fact, if it did, if the person's main focus was on having money, it is unlikely they would have money. The Lamborghini or big house are not the game. They are the rewards of the game. They are the rewards of value being created and then captured.

All successful businesses create value.

PART 6

Next

For You

The Money Context Vs. The Value Context

Why should you be interested in looking at the world from the context of value rather than the context of money?

Well, from a value-based context, your experience of life will be different, but also your effectiveness in life will be different.

Ideally, you want to be able to look at the world from both contexts, depending on what it is you want to be effective in.

There are a few things to realise about the two different views.

Control vs. Creation

Money gives control. Value gives creation.

When you are looking at the world from a context of money, it will usually be in an attempt to control something. This isn't a bad thing. Everyone needs a degree of control in life. Also, if you want to create anything on a large scale, you are going to need to be able to control the resources to do it. Money is a very effective way of doing that.

Additionally, the people with the most money tend to have the most power in society. The ability to control the resources effectively can greatly impact people's lives. If you want to have a lot of power and influence, you will need the ability to either manage money or have great people do it for you.

The energy of money is one of restriction and constraint.

Value, on the other hand, is about creativity. When you are looking at the world from a context of value, there is an experience of abundance. That is because there actually *is* abundance. There is no limit to the amount of value that can be created. Value does not need to be controlled. Even by just passing an item from one person to another, value can be created. Wealth is infinite.

Successful entrepreneurs are people who are masters of creating value. It may look like they are masterful with money, but often they aren't. It is just that they are great at creating value. As we saw in our light bulb example earlier, the people who end up with the most money are the ones who create the most value.

Ideally, of course, it makes sense to be able to operate from either context. There are times when it will create more value to operate in the realm of money, and times when it will create more value to operate in the realm of value. The ability to switch is very powerful. Especially when you don't yet have the resources to hire others who can bring their skills.

Other interesting differences between the two contexts are:

Winning & Losing vs. Winning & Winning

In the world of money, one person wins.

If we look financially at any transaction, there is going to be a winner and there is going to be a loser. This has a real impact on how people experience interacting with each other. If I am going to trade with you, and I feel one of us is going to be better off after the trade, I want to make sure it is going to be me. It often leads to competitiveness, deceit, manipulation and mistrust. These relationships do not last long.

In the world of value, however, both people win. This has a completely different feel. If I am trading with someone from the point of view of value, there is openness, partnership, honesty and trust. If both parties experience being better off after the transaction, there is no need for competitiveness. In fact, the longer we can keep the relationship going, the better. These relationships can last for years.

Inspiration

I know people can be inspired by being wealthy, but acquiring money itself doesn't really inspire anyone. That is why people are so often illusive if asked how much money they earn. It is not something of which most people are openly proud. People are excited if acquiring the money means you are winning a game, making a difference, or performing better. However, they are not usually inspired by the financial aspect alone.

This is one of the reasons why companies do not advertise to their customers how much profit they "make". Making a bucket for 30¢ and selling it for 50¢ doesn't inspire people. It doesn't increase anyone's capacity to experience life.

Value, however, is inspiring.

Providing clean water for a village that has none is inspiring. If, in order to do this, you sell a bucket for 50¢, which will enable a family to carry water to keep themselves alive, then great. Even if it costs 30¢ to make the bucket and requires the other 20¢ as profit to incentivise investors. It increases the wealth of humanity. The value you are creating by selling buckets to enable you to go on providing clean drinking water is inspiring.

Freedom

When you alter your context for wealth from a money-based view to a value-based view, you will experience a shift in your relationship to the world. You will have less need to control and will have an experience of abundance. Even when the value you are talking about is "value as money", you will experience it differently. Money then becomes a tool to create wealth, not something that is in the way of creating wealth.

There will be a freedom you will not have experienced before. No matter if you have lots of money or not, you will experience being financially free. This is true financial freedom.

Living In A Money-Focussed World

As you become more value aware, you will notice things in the media and in your community that no longer make sense to you. You will become aware of the amount of attention people put into conversations about money ("making money", etc.) and how little attention people give to value and the creation of value. You will also begin to experience that much of this attention on money has little impact on people's wealth.

You now have a depth of understanding that will give you a deeper insight into how the world works.

Remember that others are not wrong.

They are just in a different context. When you look at the world from the context of money, things look a certain way. The world appears as competitive, constraining, restrictive, controlled and limited, and the conversations in the world often reflect this.

Watch out that you don't get pulled back into that context. It will take effort because most of the people around you will be in that context.

With practice, however, you will be able to bring yourself back to a value-based context more and more quickly. Once you get used to experiencing the creativity and freedom of living from a value-based context, the other context just won't "feel right" to you anymore.

You are not alone. More and more people are becoming proactive in asking themselves what is the value of the choices they are making.

The world is changing, and one of my aims in writing this book is to help accelerate that change.

Value-Based Living

The distinctions of value as described in this book are not something that are only going to impact one area of your life. It doesn't matter what area you start with. It will filter through to the other areas.

Whether you are a homemaker wanting to create more value for your partner or children, an employee wanting to get in touch with your own value to help you forward your career, a small business owner wanting to become more effective at creating value for yourself and your customers, or the CEO of a multinational wanting to become more effective at creating value for your stakeholders, the access is the same.

1. Become more aware of value and the trades you are making.
Start with one area of life. As you become more aware of the trades you are making in that area, allow yourself to consider trades you are making in other areas of your life. After a while, it will happen naturally. Allow yourself to notice the trades other people are making. Write down the transaction (e.g. "I trade 'value as money' for 'value as food'"). The more aware you become of value, the better. The deeper you look into the transactions, the better. The trades you make when you buy lunch. The trades you make in your relationship. In your company. With your staff. What currencies are you trading?

It is not important what you write down. What is important is that you look and write something down. The exercise itself will increase your awareness.

Do this exercise once a day for a month. It will massively alter your wealth.

2. Look at where you are creating value.
Notice the trades you are making and work out how both parties are better off. Become responsible for the value you are already creating. As your awareness of value creation increases, you will see opportunities to create value that you have never seen before. You will also see relationships where no value is being created and you will gradually move towards relationships where value is created. Your business or your job will alter as you are drawn to more value creating activities and start to increase the value you are creating.

3. Become responsible for capturing value.

Remember, you have a responsibility to capture value. The better you get at creating and capturing value, the more you will move up the ladder, and the more opportunities you will have to create and capture value. The people you are associating with will be others who are also creating and capturing value. By ensuring you continue to capture value, you will have more resources to create even more value. If you are a business person, you have a responsibility to capture value so that you can keep creating value for your stakeholders and the world at large.

Value flows to those who know what to do with it.

Connecting With You

If you have been living in the western world for much of your life, you have likely been bombarded by information about what currencies should be important to you. You may have ended up with a life which has a great deal of resources, just not the ones that you really value.

Society can put a lot of pressure on people to perform. I understand it makes things much easier to manage if we all act the same, and it is much less threatening to others if we act like they do. However, it doesn't always create the most value.

Personally, I hate living like this. The more I connect with who I really am, and the more I give myself permission to live according to what I value, the more others seem to be drawn to me.

When I live according to others' values, I feel dead. When I live according to my values, I feel alive. My passion gets expressed in life. I don't think it matters what the values are. What matters is that we live by our own values.

It can be difficult to operate this way. Most of us have grown up with a great deal of attention focused on who we want to be and little attention focused on who we are.

Who we want to be can be different from how our life looks. Who we often want to be is someone successful who fits in and is respected. Often, we suppress who we really are so we can fit in.

I would recommend you stop doing that.

Life will never go well that way. You will never win at a game you don't really want to play.

Why would you win? Winning at a game you don't really want to play will just lead you further and further from the life you really want.

This is the reason many people experience sabotaging themselves in life. It is not that you are sabotaging yourself, it is that you are stopping yourself from going down a route that is not for you.

One of the areas I have struggled to be responsible for in my own life has been my relationship to relationships. I have never connected with being in structured, exclusive relationships. They always felt very constrained for me. I would meet someone I really liked, then end up in a "relationship" with them. I would then act a certain way because I was in a "relationship" with them and would also be expected to act a certain way with others. At some point, I would begin to resent this and try to find a way out of the relationship. Usually this involved "splitting up" with a person I really cared about, and often I would be expected not to speak to them again.

It is a strange cycle that doesn't represent how relationships occur for me.

In reality, relationships occur for me as much more dynamic than that. At any time, there are lots of people I am in relationships with. Some people I do business with. Others I may play squash with, be friends with or explore intimacy with. I get mentally why people are drawn to exclusive relationships, but, in my heart, they don't make sense.

The point of this story is not that one type of relationship is better than another. Exclusivity can provide an incredible amount of value for a relationship, and also children, families and the community around that relationship.

The point is, life will not start really working for you until you are honest about the life that you want to live.

I have recently become much more interested in what value I provide in my relationships. What is important to the people who want to spend time with me? What is important for me that makes me want to spend time with them? It has created a great deal more harmony and allowed me to focus on what is important to me and to others.

For the World

Responsibility

In current times, there is a great deal of fight-back against business owners, corporations and capitalism in general.

It is very easy to blame business owners, and those who have a great deal of money, for the problems in society. Blaming them, however, is unlikely to help. Business owners are needed to create positive impact in society.

To make valuable changes to society, instead of fighting against each other, people who want to make a difference need to work in partnership with the business community.

Let's talk about responsibility.

In society, we are often calling for people to be more responsible. What this generally means is that we want someone to take the blame for something bad that has happened.

We want "rich" people to be responsible for people who are dying of hunger. We want oil companies to be responsible for the environment. I understand. We want people to account for the impact of their actions.

The problem is, I rarely hear anyone calling for business owners to be responsible for the value they *create*. I have never heard anyone acknowledge the head of an oil company for the hundreds of millions of lives that are positively altered as a result of fuel in their cars, ships, aeroplanes or machinery.

Responsibility is not a one-sided coin. There are only levels of being responsible, and you can't be responsible for the things that don't go well without also being responsible for the things that do go well.

In order to try to get people to be more responsible, however, we want them to look at the negative impact of where they are not being responsible.

That doesn't cause any change, though. Nobody wants to be responsible for the bad stuff.

That is why the blame gets passed around.

The way to convince people to become more responsible is to have them take responsibility for the positive impact they can have. When someone becomes responsible for the positive impact they have on society, they increase their overall capacity for responsibility, allowing them, in turn, to become responsible for the negative impact of their actions.

When people are connected to the difference they make, they naturally want to amplify that.

It works that way for all of us, and it works that way for business owners. This is the same conversation that we had earlier about how staff are more effective in a value-based business culture. The key is for people to experience the value they create.

If you want business leaders to take more responsibility in society, acknowledge them for the positive impact they are having. For the value they are already creating.

When a person starts to understand that business is about creating value and not making money – and that if they are "making money" they are already creating value – then it becomes possible to look at how they can create the same value, or greater value, with less negative impact.

It may not happen overnight, but this is the change that needs to happen. That is how business can and will alter society. We don't need to change from a capitalist society, we just need to change our understanding of what capitalism is actually about.

Shared Value

In 2006, Michael E. Porter and Mark R. Kramer, two leading authorities of the business world, wrote an article called *Strategy and Society: The Link between Competitive Advantage and Corporate Social Responsibility*. In 2011, the article was followed up with another titled *Creating Shared Value: Redefining Capitalism and the Role of the Corporation in Society*. These articles explore the relationship between business and society and how they are dependant on each other – hence the name Shared Value.

In 2012, it was announced that a Shared Value Initiative would be established as part of the Clinton Global Initiative. Since then, companies such as Nestle, HP, CJ Group, Chevron, Intel, Verizon and Deloitte have worked with the Shared Value Initiative to explore increasing the positive impact of their business.

Although not yet integrated into common business practice, the ideas explored in both articles have greatly forwarded the conversation for the role of business in society. I believe there is great deal more benefit to be gained from exploring shared value.

Benefit Corporations

In April 2010, Maryland became the first state in the U.S. to pass benefit corporation legislation. This legislation allows for the creation of a new type of business entity called a benefit corporation (or B-Corporation). Previously, businesses have been categorized as a profit making entity (a traditional business) or a non-profit making entity (a not for profit).

This new classification allows a business to be set up as a profit making entity that is also committed to maximising the value it creates for other stakeholders.

Since 2010, 28 U.S. states have passed this legislation and, although each country outside the U.S. will deal with the issue of legislation individually, the movement has spread further throughout the world.

Although not directly connected to the U.S. legislation, a certification process has been created through an entity called B-labs. Any type of entity, from a small business to a large corporation, can apply for certification as a B-Corporation. However, it must meet specific criteria regarding social and environmental impact.

At the time of writing this book, there are 1203 certified B-Corporations spread over 38 countries and 121 industries.

Whether the B-Corporation takes hold and creates a seismic shift in how business owners operate is yet to be seen.

One thing I am sure about, however, the movement is bringing attention to the conversation that business is not only about profit. Becoming a B-Corporation may be a stage in raising the consciousness of some business owners — and raising consciousness is always a good thing.

Philanthropy

I have never had a strong relationship to giving money to charity. Although I have done it, and believe it can make a big difference, I first ask myself the question, "Is giving money going to create value or not?"

For some problems, giving money can work very well.

There are times when someone needs urgent emergency attention. Famine, floods, wartime issues and money may assist in bringing together the resources to get people through these times. Fortunately, there are agencies that are highly effective at doing that.

For dealing with long term problems, however, simply giving money never seemed to me to be a good solution. I am, however, very interested in how we can raise the living standards of those who are the poorest in the world.

How do we raise their experience of life?

What needs to happen to have whole communities raise their own standards of living?

I have heard numerous stories of initiatives that are not effective in creating the result for which they were intended. I believe the problem often comes from people outside of the community trying to fix the problem, but problems can rarely be dealt with that way.

Someone once said to me, "Helping people often leaves them helpless".

To raise the wealth of a community, I believe the people in the community need to experience themselves as the ones creating value. The more that people in the community know themselves as able to create value, the more effective they become at solving problems. To cause sustainable growth in low socio-economic communities, there needs to be value created within that community itself.

This doesn't mean that the communities cannot be supported to connect with their own value and capitalise on creating value inside and/or outside their community. They can.

Microfunding

Microfunding, microfinance, microcredit and crowdfunding can greatly impact a community's ability to create value. As we discussed earlier, that is what money does. It is a tool that amplifies our ability to trade, and the easier it is to trade, the easier it is to create wealth.

When there is a lack of money available in a community, trading becomes much harder. When there is less trading, there is less value getting created. It is part of the cycle of poverty.

Personally, I love microfunding. I believe it is part of the access to long term prosperity in the lowest socio-economic communities. It may not provide a quick fix to wealth, but it certainly increases a community's ability to create wealth.

When you fund a business venture in a new community (using any of the methods mentioned above), you support a marketplace. A marketplace which doesn't just benefit the person you loaned funds to. It affects the community as a whole. Every person the borrower trades with also increases their wealth.

Remember, the purpose of loaning money is not to give the farmer/cobbler/carpenter money. It is to stimulate trade. By loaning the money, the person has to trade to be able to pay back the loan, and through trading, the whole community benefits.

Even if the business fails, there is educational value provided to the community. Whether it be a first world country or a third world country, most entrepreneurs fail at some point. It is all part of the apprenticeship.

This is one of the incredible things about money. Now, in a couple of minutes on the internet, you can select an entrepreneur in a third world country on sites such as Kiva.org and loan him $25 to buy some chickens. Without money, it would be practically impossible to provide resources to someone overseas.

Giving

Although the benefits to the receiver of philanthropy will vary according to the circumstances, one thing is clear: when there is a conversation for philanthropy, there is great benefit for the giver. I don't mean this in a shallow, egotistical, selfish way. I mean genuine value.

When a person or organisation looks outside of themselves in an effort to make a difference with someone else, it is a good thing. The looking itself creates value. That is why just giving money blindly has never appealed to me. What will solve the problems of the world is people getting interested in the problems of the world.

It does not take a lot to get by in life today. We don't have to fight off sabre tooth tigers, struggle through swamps to find food, or drive a millstone to mill grain. We can hand over a few dollars at the local supermarket and walk out with a loaf of bread and some cold ham.

We have it pretty good.

People can often be thought of as being selfish. However, in my experience, people are bored.

When people experience making a difference for others, they end up much more effective in life. It is often the ability to have impact beyond yourself that creates freedom and inspiration.

The Wealth Gap

"The top 1% of the world population controls 40% of the world's wealth."

One of the things I often read, particularly when musing through the posts of some in my Facebook community, is how the top 40% of the world's wealth is controlled by the top 1% of the world's population. There is usually also a comment about how corporations, and the rich people who control the corporations, are the enemies of society.

This is an interesting view.

I believe this view of corporations and the wealthy is usually counter-productive to the person who is making the statement. Corporations are, after all, made up of people. The people who control corporations are the people who have the power to *alter* the course of society.

Fighting the people who we think are causing the problem rarely works. We need to befriend the people who we think are causing the problem. They are often the access to dealing with the problem.

Let's look at a number of things about this.

1. Because the top 1% control 40% of the world's wealth, it does not mean that they are holding 40% the world's wealth. There is a difference between controlling an asset and holding an asset. Money gives a measure of control, but that is not the actual wealth. The top 1% do not hold 40% of the worlds:
   a. Food
   b. Water
   c. Real Estate

Or other similar assets.

2. If they have had an abundance of money for a period of time, it is likely they have created value, and have continued to create value. They cannot stay wealthy in a world that is creating value without also creating value. Even if they have $100

million in a bank account paying 4% interest, they are creating value. The $100 million will be loaned out to someone who will use it to create more value than if the $100 million were in a box.

3. Many of the people who have a lot of money are business people. They do not have 1% of the wealth hoarded under their mattresses. It will be controlling business assets and those businesses assets will be creating value.

4. If the control is taken from the rich and people who run corporations, who do we give it to? This is not food we are talking about – this is the control of food. Do we want to redistribute money from the 1% of the population with the most money and give it to the 1% with the least money? Do we take it from the people who have the most experience in creating value and give it to the people who have the least experience in creating value? This will not work. The money will quickly flow again to the people who have the most experience in creating value.

It is not money that we want to redistribute. This is a mistake that comes from the current conversations that wealth is money. It is the assets that money can control that we want to redistribute.

This is more difficult than you can imagine.

As Bob Geldof found out after Live Aid, money did not have the power to make the difference he thought. Starving people need food and fresh water, not money. Money can often not ensure food and fresh water.

If this were the case, world hunger would have ceased decades ago. There are many committed people in the world with a great deal of resources who are able to impact the redistribution of money. Plenty of smart people are working on this task.

They know, however, that only redistributing money will not make the difference.

5. I think the problem is that the top 1% are not given credit for the

positive impact they have on society and are, therefore, not really connected with their own capacity to amplify/accentuate that impact. If the top 1% become more connected to their capacity to make a difference, I believe it is inevitable that they will look for ways to become more efficient at making that difference.

This is already happening with some of the richest people in the world.

In the year 2000, two of the richest people in the world, Bill and Melinda Gates, created their own foundation. The foundation was created to provide resources to impact major issues in the world including healthcare and extreme poverty (globally), and to expand educational opportunities and access to information technology (in the U.S.). So far, they have contributed US$42.3 billion to the trust and plan to donate 95% of their wealth (currently $79.2 billion) to charity.

Warren Buffett (another of the world's richest people) has said he will give 99% of his wealth (currently US$73 billion) to charity. Already, 83% has been pledged to the Bill & Melinda Gates Foundation.

The "Gates-Buffett Giving Pledge" was then designed to invite others to donate at least 50% of their wealth over their lifetime.

Since that time, there have been over a hundred more signatories from some of the world's wealthiest people, including Mark Zuckerberg and Richard Branson. For more information, check out https://en.wikipedia.org/wiki/The_Giving_Pledge.

6. As much as there is inequality of the distribution of money, there is a real opportunity in this.

In the hands of the right people, money can be incredibly powerful. If I were someone who wanted to raise funds, I would much prefer to have one conversation that donated $30 billion, than to have 3 billion conversations that donate $10 each.

Money flowing to the top 1% is not the problem. The money

is in the hands of people who know how to create value. People who know how to manage assets. How to build businesses. With a relatively small increase in consciousness, these people can have a massive impact on society.

It Is On Us

As much as I would like to leave the problems of the world in the hands of the top 1%, I don't think that is going to cut it. It will take more than a raising of the consciousness of the top 1%.

The access to wealth is to create value, and that has to happen at ground level. It happens between you and me. Between you and your partner. Between you and your family. Between you and your friends. Between you and your employer. Between you and your clients. Between you and the strangers that you can now start a conversation with because that relationship, in itself, will provide an access to creating value. All of this you can do, no matter how much money you have.

Today is the 28th December.

This year, for Christmas, I wanted to experience, and to have my children experience, giving to others as well as receiving. I asked Ali to contact some welfare agencies to see if we could assist them in some way on Christmas morning. As we had children, however, she was told it would not be possible.

Ali then contacted the local old folks' home and asked if we could come and sing some carols to the residents. At 11am Christmas morning, after the children had opened their presents, the residents of the old folks' home were wheeled into their television room and greeted by Ali giving out chocolates. With our children, we then entertained the residents for 30 minutes with our renditions of Christmas carols.

It was a great experience that created value for both the residents and for our family.

The faces of the residents as we sang were incredibly moving.

It was also great to see my kids being a contribution.

This small gesture was one of the highlights of my year.

As I have said, becoming aware of your own capacity to create value is essential to creating wealth for you and for others. Start with small gestures in your life right now. It can greatly accentuate your experience of your own value. As you create value, you become more responsible for your capacity to create value. It happens naturally.

To end hunger and famine in Africa, it will take more than money. It will take creative thought to look at the current political climate and the assets that people currently have, and work out how to best make use of them to impact the problem.

Remember, monetary growth has no value to the world. It is a bi-product of creating value. Creating value is what increases the wealth of the planet. It is what expands yours and others' capacity to experience life. It is what increases wealth.

Focus on this and the world will be a better place for us all.

Congratulations!

You have started a journey to become a master of value creation.

To continue the conversation

Visit www.terencesweeney.com/updateme and register your details.
I will keep you up to date with conversations and other resources I
am creating.

Business Advisory & Consulting

To discuss how I can help you bring the distinctions of value creation
to your organisation, call or email me.
Visit www.terencesweeney.com for contact details.

To have me speak at your organisation

I love to give keynotes and create conversations that impact both the
business community and the world at large. To discus your needs
call or email me. Visit www.terencesweeney.com for contact details.

Further resources

Visit www.terencesweeney.com/resources for resources to assist
you in developing your awareness of value.

www.terencesweeney.com

Glossary of Terms

B Corporation - A for-profit corporate entity whose legally defined goals include positive impact on society and the environment.

Business - An entity which brings together resources with the intention of creating value. A business is also a type of marketplace.

Currency - An area of life in which you hold value and that can be traded with or for.

Diminishing Usefulness - As the quantity of a currency increases, the usefulness of each additional amount of that currency decreases.

Entrepreneur - A person who can identify opportunities to create value and develop it into a business structure which continues to create and capture value.

Gold Standard - The system by which the value of a currency was defined in terms of gold, for which the currency could be exchanged.

Marketplace - Any arena where currencies are traded.

Micro-funding - The lending of very small amounts of money at low interest, especially to a start-up company or self-employed person.

Money -
1. A current medium of exchange – usually in the form of coins and banknotes.

2. A store of value.

3. A unit of account.

Obsession - Over-valuing a particular currency due to programming or neurosis.

Relationship - The connection which allows two parties to trade value.

Shared Value - Shared value is a management strategy designed to support a company in creating measurable business value by identifying and addressing social problems that intersect with their business.

Trading - Exchanging value in one currency for value in another currency.

Value - The capacity of an item or service to increase your experience of life.

Value Awareness - Being aware of the value of a particular product, service, currency or trade.

Value Capture - The portion of the created value that you retain as a result of a trade.

Value Creation - A trade in which all parties are better off after the trade than before.

Value Extraction - When one party in a trade captures more value than is being created by the trade. Value extraction is unsustainable.

Wealth - An abundance of resources in the currencies that are important to you.

Resources

Links

Free Hugs   https://youtu.be/DugeQ6vkC6Y

Lean Thinking   Book by Eric Ries-
http://theleanstartup.com/

Simon Sinek   "Start With Why"-
https://youtu.be/sioZd3AxmnE

Michael E. Porter & Mark R. Kramer

"Strategy and Society: The Link between Competitive Advantage and Corporate Social Responsibility"

https://hbr.org/2006/12/strategy-and-society-the-link-between-competitive-advantage-and-corporate-social-responsibility

"Creating Shared Value: Redefining Capitalism and the Role of the Corporation in Society"

https://hbr.org/2011/01/the-big-idea-creating-shared-value

The Shared Value Initiative http://sharedvalue.org/

B Corporation http://www.bcorporation.net/

The Giving Pledge https://en.wikipedia.org/wiki/The_Giving_Pledge

Acknowledgments

I have been fortunate to have met many great people over the years. Some who have contributed greatly and travelled far with me. Others who may have only contributed a few words; however, they were words that expanded my world.

I would like to express thanks:

To Ali for always telling me how great I am, mostly when I am not. To my children Jack, Jessica, Luke and Chloe, for whom I am constantly having to step up my game. To my father, Terry, and my mother, Catherine, for starting me off on the journey, and for always being available. To my brother, Craig, and my sister, Paula, for the growing we did together, and the learning along the way.

The following people have all contributed in some way to this book becoming available:

Cathy Elliot, Francis Foster, Moshe Goldberg, Paul Berry, Rachael Kane, Noni Turner, Hugh Bevage, John Assaraf, Esther Hicks, Tim Longhurst, Darren Hill, Peter Cook, Matt Church, Natasa Denman, Emily Gowor, Ocean Reeve and Ben Wicks.

To Miriam Ercole, Christie Pinto, Julian McLucas, Celia Taylor and James McCracken. Thank you for your feedback on the manuscript.

To the following people, our universes connected when needed: Pushkar Gogia, Simon Burke, Greg Ryan, Nev Bray and the rest of the Brays.

Finally, to all of the countless others who, in some way, had me feel that I had something to contribute to the world.

With love and appreciation,

Terence Sweeney

About Terence Sweeney

In Business...

Terence Sweeney has extensive hands on experience in business. From starting up his first business at age 21, he has successfully been involved in start-ups, led struggling businesses through to success and been CEO of his own company. Terence now writes, speaks and consults to business about the distinctions of value creation.

Terence is an associate member of the National Speakers Association of Australia and has a Bachelor of Applied Science (I.T.) with distinction.

In Life...

Terence has been exploring how people work for his entire life. It is his biggest passion. It started as a means to challenge his own performance, and has naturally led to making a difference with others. Along the way, Terence has led training and development seminars, and has over 10 years' experience in coaching people who are interested in high performance and fulfilment.

Terence is an APSI Level 1 Ski-Instructor, a PADI Scuba Dive-Master and, when at home, can often be found "dancing like a dad" with one of his four children.

To stay connected with Terence visit:

www.terencesweeney.com

www.ingramcontent.com/pod-product-compliance
Lightning Source LLC
Chambersburg PA
CBHW070727220326
41598CB00024BA/3339